Cambridge Elements

Elements in Shakespeare and Text
edited by
Claire M. L. Bourne
The Pennsylvania State University
Rory Loughnane
University of Kent

COLLABORATION, TECHNOLOGIES, AND THE HISTORY OF SHAKESPEAREAN BIBLIOGRAPHY

Heidi Craig
University of Toronto

Laura Estill
St. Francis Xavier University

Kris L. May
Texas A&M University

Dorothy Todd
Texas A&M University

Shaftesbury Road, Cambridge CB2 8EA, United Kingdom

One Liberty Plaza, 20th Floor, New York, NY 10006, USA

477 Williamstown Road, Port Melbourne, VIC 3207, Australia

314–321, 3rd Floor, Plot 3, Splendor Forum, Jasola District Centre,
New Delhi – 110025, India

Cambridge University Press is part of Cambridge University Press & Assessment,
a department of the University of Cambridge.

We share the University's mission to contribute to society through the pursuit of
education, learning and research at the highest international levels of excellence.

www.cambridge.org
Information on this title: www.cambridge.org/9781009614115

DOI: 10.1017/9781009614108

© Heidi Craig, Laura Estill, Kris L. May, and Dorothy Todd 2026

This publication is in copyright. Subject to statutory exception and to the provisions
of relevant collective licensing agreements, with the exception of the Creative Commons version the link
for which is provided below, no reproduction of any part may take place without the written permission of
Cambridge University Press & Assessment.

An online version of this work is published at doi.org/10.1017/9781009614108 under a Creative
Commons Open Access license CC-BY-NC 4.0 which permits re-use, distribution and reproduction
in any medium for non-commercial purposes providing appropriate credit to the original work is
given and any changes made are indicated. To view a copy of this license visit
https://creativecommons.org/licenses/by-nc/4.0

When citing this work, please include a reference to the DOI 10.1017/9781009614108

First published 2026

A catalogue record for this publication is available from the British Library

A Cataloging-in-Publication data record for this Element is available from the Library of Congress

ISBN 978-1-009-61411-5 Paperback
ISSN 2754-4257 (online)
ISSN 2754-4249 (print)

Additional resources for this publication at www.cambridge.org/Estill

Cambridge University Press & Assessment has no responsibility for the persistence
or accuracy of URLs for external or third-party internet websites referred to in this
publication and does not guarantee that any content on such websites is, or will
remain, accurate or appropriate.

For EU product safety concerns, contact us at Calle de José Abascal, 56, 1°, 28003 Madrid, Spain, or
email eugpsr@cambridge.org

Collaboration, Technologies, and the History of Shakespearean Bibliography

Elements in Shakespeare and Text

DOI: 10.1017/9781009614108
First published online: March 2026

Heidi Craig
University of Toronto

Laura Estill
St. Francis Xavier University

Kris L. May
Texas A&M University

Dorothy Todd
Texas A&M University

Author for correspondence: Laura Estill, lestill@stfx.ca

ABSTRACT: This Element traces the history of Shakespearean bibliography from its earliest days to the present. With an emphasis on how we enumerate and find scholarship about Shakespeare, this Element argues that understanding bibliographies is foundational to how we research Shakespeare. From early modern catalogs of Shakespeare plays, to early bibliographers such as Albert Cohn (1827–1905) and William Jaggard (1868–1947), to present-day digital projects such as the online *World Shakespeare Bibliography*, this Element underscores how the taxonomic organization, ambit, and media of enumerative Shakespearean bibliography projects directly impact how scholars value and can use these resources. Ultimately, this Element asks us to rethink our assumptions about Shakespearean bibliography by foregrounding the labor, collaboration, technological innovations, and critical decisions that go into creating and sustaining bibliographies at all stages. This title is also available as Open Access on Cambridge Core.

KEYWORDS: Shakespeare, bibliography, literary studies, history of Shakespeare studies, digital humanities

© Heidi Craig, Laura Estill, Kris L. May, and Dorothy Todd 2026

ISBNs: 9781009614115 (PB), 9781009614108 (OC)
ISSNs: 2754-4257 (online), 2754-4249 (print)

Contents

Introduction: Enumerative Bibliography as the Foundation
of Shakespeare Scholarship 1

1 Shakespearean List-Making from Francis Meres
   to William Jaggard 5

2 German Traditions of Shakespeare Bibliography:
   Format, Categories, Meaning 16

3 *Shakespeare Association Bulletin* and *Shakespeare
   Quarterly*: Anglo-American Annual Shakespeare
   Bibliographies 38

4 Regional Shakespeare Bibliographies: Case Studies
   in Scope and Scholarly Attention 56

5 Collaboration and Technology in the *World
   Shakespeare Bibliography* 73

Coda: Looking Forward 105

Introduction: Enumerative Bibliography as the Foundation of Shakespeare Scholarship

> "A lifetime would not suffice to draw up a complete bibliography of the studies related to Shakespeare." – René Hainaux, "Shakespeare Bibliography"[1]

It has been over a century since Clark S. Northup advocated for a systematic, comprehensive bibliography of Shakespeare.[2] Since then, hundreds of thousands of articles, chapters, and monographs about Shakespeare have come to press, and bibliographers struggle to keep up. Our Element addresses the changing parameters of Shakespearean bibliography by exploring its multifaceted history; by recovering the labor of the bibliographers that underpins our scholarship; and by tracing the changing technologies and institutions that shape the structures and strictures of how we undertake bibliography – and therefore research – today.

It was not long after Shakespeare's plays were first published that individuals attempted to catalog and list them. Consider, for instance, that Francis Meres's oft-cited *Palladis Tamia* (1598) lists titles of Shakespeare's plays to exemplify his skill as a writer of both tragedy and comedy and to compare him positively to his literary predecessors and contemporaries. In the interest of space and relevance, apart from sixteenth- and seventeenth-century lists of Shakespeare's works, this Element does not address more recent lists of editions and copies of Shakespeare's plays, for instance, of the kind created by Henrietta C. Bartlett in the early twentieth century; by

---

[1] René Hainaux, "Shakespearian Bibliography | Bibliographie shakesperienne," *Le Théâtre Dans Le Monde* (1964): 127–34, 127.

[2] Clark S. Northup, "On the Bibliography of Shakespeare," *The Journal of English and Germanic Philology* 11, no. 2 (1912): 218–30. Northup later published a bibliography of existing lists: "Shakespeare Bibliographies and Reference Lists," *Papers of the Bibliographical Society of America* 10, no. 2 (1916): 92–100, www.jstor.org/stable/45275761, as well as the more expansive *A Register of Bibliographies of the English Language and Literature*, with contributions by Joseph Quincy Adams and Andrew Keogh (Oxford University Press, 1825).

Adam G. Hooks and Zachary Lesser in the *Shakespeare Census*, a digital take on Bartlett's census; and by Andrew Murphy's *Shakespeare in Print*, which aims to list all editions of Shakespeare's works up to its date of publication.[3] Instead, it focuses on lists of secondary scholarship on Shakespeare. We do not take it upon ourselves to define what scholarship is – rather, those intrepid bibliographers whose works we discuss set the scope of what counts as scholarship for each of their projects.

Making lists of texts – the foundation of enumerative bibliography and the basis of research from antiquity – is a response to a seeming superabundance of material.[4] That there is "too much to know" about Shakespeare has been a persistent sentiment for at least two centuries. As Robert Southey observed in 1804 (in response to Issac Reed's twenty-one volume edition of Shakespeare's complete works published in 1803): "Comments upon Shakespeare keep pace with the National Debt, and will at last become equally insufferable and out of fashion; yet I should like to see his book, and would buy it if I could."[5,6] Southey's ambivalence conveys a sense of the overwhelming number of Shakespeare editions and scholarship by the early nineteenth century and also readers' insatiable appetites for that seeming glut. Lists allow us to reconcile this sense of bibliographical excess with intellectual desire, as they are a time-efficient way to record and process lots of information.[7] Indeed, it is striking how

[3] For more on Henrietta C. Bartlett's census of Shakespeare editions, see Eve Houghton's "Private Owners, Public Books: Henrietta Bartlett's Feminist Bibliography," *The Papers of the Bibliographical Society of America* 116, no. 4 (December 2022): 567–87. See also Adam G. Hooks and Zachary Lesser, *The Shakespeare Census*, shakespearecensus.org/; and Andrew D. Murphy, *Shakespeare in Print*, 2nd ed. (Cambridge University Press, 2021).

[4] Ann Blair, Too Much to Know: Managing Scholarly Information Before the Modern Age (Yale University Press, 2010).

[5] Robert Southey, "[Letter] To Grosvenor C. Bedford, Esq." February 16, 1804 in *The Life and Correspondence of Robert Southey*, Vol. 2, ed. Charles Cuthbert Southey (London: Longman, Brown, Green & Longmans, 1849–50), 260.

[6] Southey, "[Letter] To Grosvenor C. Bedford," 260.

[7] Roman Alexander Barton, Julia Böckling, Sarah Link, and Anne Rüggemeier, "Introduction: Epistemic and Artistic List-Making," in *Forms of List-Making:*

much enduring scholarship on early modern drama, especially Shakespeare, is itself in lists, which even in their pared-down versions cannot include all relevant material.

In analog contexts, the compulsion to enumerate led to self-referential and meta-reference works such as Theodore Besterman's *A World Bibliography of Bibliographies (And of Bibliographical Catalogues, Calendars, Abstracts, Digests, Indexes and the Like)*, which was compiled from 1939 to 1955 with supplements into the late twentieth century.[8] Shakespearean bibliography thus participates in the genre's self-referential nature – Shakespeare bibliographies that aim at comprehensiveness must cite other Shakespeare bibliographies – and also its recursiveness, as each bibliography builds on, extends, and perpetuates the genre: it's bibliographies all the way down.

The importance of lists to literary scholarship should be understood in the context of the discipline of enumerative bibliography: that is, purposeful list-making that was intended to be comprehensive and usable for scholarship by activating particular taxonomies or principles of organization. As the later sections in this Element detail, enumerative bibliographies take many forms: stand-alone codices designed to capture all scholarship to date, but which themselves quickly became outdated; print periodical bibliographies that offer regular updates but were not themselves comprehensive; and later, digital bibliographies, which offer entirely new affordances and can present the illusion of completeness. While the ideals that enumerative bibliographers bring to their work on Shakespeare are often the same, the choices they make and contexts in which they make them (including historical, geographical, and technological) have determined the scope and contents of the bibliographies themselves. In this way, our Element explores how these bibliographies offer scholar-users different means of navigation, searchability, and, especially, usability.

Epistemic, Literary, and Visual Enumeration, eds. Barton, Böckling, Link, Rüggemeier (Palgrave Macmillan, 2022), 1–s24, 5.

[8] Thomas Besterman, *A World Bibliography of Bibliographies (And of Bibliographical Catalogues, Calendars, Abstracts, Digests, Indexes and the Like)* (Edwards Brothers, 1939).

Section 1 explores early practices of Shakespearean list-making in the sixteenth and seventeenth centuries and the cultural impulses that underlay them, as well as the emergence of modern conventions of enumerative bibliography (i.e., comprehensive and sorted lists intended for scholarly use) in the nineteenth century. Section 2 draws on German traditions of Shakespeare bibliography to emphasize the different affordances of periodical publication (in, for instance, the *Shakespeare Jahrbuch*) and standalone bibliographies. We offer specific examples of how early bibliographers positioned their work and how early scholars around the world used these bibliographies to undertake research. Section 3 sheds light on the annual bibliographies produced by *Shakespeare Quarterly* (*SQ*) and its direct predecessor, the *Shakespeare Association Bulletin* (*SAB*), a journal created in 1924 by the Shakespeare Association of America. As this bibliography evolved from the *Shakespeare Association Bulletin*'s annual bibliography, to *SQ*'s *World Shakespeare Bibliography* (*WSB*), to the *WSB* online, through various institutional and media shifts, the bibliographers responsible for these resources attempted to compile comprehensive lists of Shakespearean scholarship. For over a century, bibliographers lamented the impossibility of the task, but also drew strength from the shared – and global – scholarly enterprise of bibliography. Building on the German and Anglo-American traditions discussed in earlier sections, Section 4 traces regional bibliographies from Japan, Spain, Canada, and South Africa to demonstrate how each emphasizes Shakespeare's regional importance as well as different national approaches to Shakespeare scholarship. Section 5 turns back to the *WSB* to show how digital technologies revolutionized enumerative Shakespeare bibliography by altering the material form of the bibliography from static to dynamic (from print to CD-ROM to digital online presence). This shift reshaped search and browse functionality, increased access to bibliographies, and expedited the speed at which bibliographies could be assembled, distributed, updated with new entries, corrected, and searched.

Shakespeare is the most-written-about literary author. His reach is truly international. The challenge of adequately (let alone accurately) cataloging the breadth and depth of Shakespeare scholarship has always been daunting, but it is also transformative: as bibliographers have grappled with exponentially growing quantities of Shakespeare scholarship, their responses have shaped the theories and practices of Shakespeare studies itself. Shakespeare studies, furthermore, is often a bellwether or test case for other areas of literary study. For bibliographical practices, specifically, Shakespeare is exceptional both because of the amount of material written about him and because scholarship about Shakespeare so often sets the stage for literary scholarship in general.

1 Shakespearean List-Making from Francis Meres to William Jaggard

Planning what would become the *World Shakespeare Bibliography*, Harrison T. Meserole and John B. Smith wrote: "Shakespeare's unique position in world literature has encouraged an unceasing and burgeoning record of publications and stage presentations and, consequently, an active bibliographical industry to control and make accessible that record."[9] The "active bibliographical industry" invoked by *WSB* editors Meserole and Smith in 1981 flourished during the twentieth century, but its roots can be traced to the late sixteenth century. As noted in the introduction, an early instance of Shakespearean bibliography appears in *Palladis Tamia* (1598), where Francis Meres listed a dozen Shakespeare plays (Figure 1).[10] Meres's list is often cited as evidence for the chronology of Shakespeare's plays. Unlike later bibliographers, however, Meres did not necessarily aim for comprehensiveness; most scholars agree that *The Taming of the Shrew* and *1, 2,* and *3 Henry VI* already existed when he published his list in 1598, even though these titles are not included. Nor was his focus solely upon Shakespeare: even though Meres is mostly read today for insights on Shakespeare's corpus and reputation in the late sixteenth century, Shakespeare is only one of many authors he names in a laundry list of classical and

---

[9] Harrison T. Meserole and John B. Smith, "'Yet There Is Method in It': The Cumulative Shakespeare Bibliography – A Product of Project Planning in the Humanities," *Perspectives in Computing* 1, no. 2 (1981): 4–11, 10n1.

[10] Francis Meres, *Palladis Tamia Wits Treasury: Being the Second Part of Wits Commonwealth* (London: Cuthbert Burbie, 1598).

The second yeare of

mong al writers to be of an honest life and vpright conuersation: to *Michael Drayton* (*quem toties honoris & amoris causa[sic] nomino*) among schollers, souldiours, Poets, and al sorts of people, is helde for a man of vertuous disposition, honest conuersation, and wel gouerned cariage, which is almost miraculous among good wits in these declining and corrupt times, when there is nothing but roguery in villanous man, & whē cheating and craftines is coūted the cleanest wit, and soundest wisedome.

As *Decius Ausonius Gallus in libr: de fig floru[m]*, penned the occurrences of ye world from the first creation of it to his time, that is, to the raigne of the Emperour *Gratian*: so *Warner* in his absolute *Albions England* hath most admirably penned the historie of his own country from *Noah* to his time, that is to the raigne of Queene *Elizabeth*: I haue heard him termd of the best wits of both our Vniuersities, our English *Homer*.

As *Euripides* is the most sententious among the Greek Poets: so is *Warner* amōg our English Poets.

As the soule of *Euphorbus* was thought to liue in *Pythagoras*: so the sweete wittie soule of *Ouid* liues in mellifluous & hony-tongued *Shakespeare*, witnes his *Venus and Adonis*, his *Lucrece*, his sugred Sonnets among

Wits Common-Wealth. 282

ng his priuate friends, &c.

As *Plautus* and *Seneca* are accounted the best for Comedy and Tragedy among the Latines: so *Shakespeare* among ye English is the most excellent in both kinds for the stage; for Comedy, witnes his *Ge[n]tleme[n] of Verona*, his *Errors*, his *Loue labors lost*, his *Loue labours wonne*, his *Midsummers night dreame*, & his *Merchant of Venice*: for Tragedy his *Richard the 2. Richard the 3. Henry the 4. King Iohn, Titus Andronicus* and his *Romeo and Iuliet*.

As *Epius Stolo* said, that the Muses would speake with *Plautus* tongue, if they would speake Latin: so I say that the Muses would speake with *Shakespeares* fine filed phrase, if they would speake English.

As *Musæus*, who wrote the loue of *Hero* and *Leander*, had two excellent schollers, *Thamaras* & *Hercules*: so hath he in England two excellent Poets, imitators of him in the same argument and subiect, *Christopher Marlow*, and *George Chapman*.

As *Ouid* saith of his worke;

Iamque opus exegi, quod nec Iouis ira, nec ignis,
Nec poterit ferrum, nec edax abolere vetustas.

And as *Horace* saith of his; *Exegi monumentum ære perennius; Regalique, situ pyramidum altius; Quod non imber edax; Non Aquilo impotens possit diruere; aut innumerabilis*

Oo2,

contemporary literary writers, from Homer and Virgil, to Spenser and Sidney, to many authors barely remembered today.

While Meres created heterogeneous lists of authors and texts to assert evaluative analogies between well-known and lesser-known writers, the mid seventeenth century saw lists deployed to enumerate a more focused category: English printed drama. In 1656 two catalogs were published claiming to list all English plays in print, both titled "Exact and perfect" catalogs of English playbooks, printed by William Rogers and Richard Ley and included with Thomas Goffe's play *The Careless Shepherdess*, and by Edward Archer included in *The Old Law* by Thomas Middleton, William Rowley, and Thomas Heywood.[11] Heidi Craig has elsewhere written about these comprehensive catalogs, arguing that these lists were not primarily commercial in nature, but rather had informational purposes.[12] The effort to list all plays by Shakespeare was part of a broader goal to comprehensively list all English playbooks. As with Meres, Shakespeare was only one of many on a list. While the 1656 comprehensive catalogs are often overlooked in examinations of early bibliography (omitted from William Jaggard's 1911 account, discussed in a following section, and receiving brief attention in Adam G. Hooks's *Selling Shakespeare*),[13] they inspired the Restoration publisher Francis Kirkman's better-known "perfect and exact" lists of all English plays, printed in 1661 and 1671, which, like their predecessors from 1656, aimed for comprehensiveness. Rounding out the century are Gerard Langbaine's bio-bibliographies of English drama, printed in the 1690s. These early

[11] "An exact and perfect Catologue of all Playes that are Printed," in *The Careless Shepherdess*, ed. Thomas Goffe (London: William Rogers and Richard Ley, 1656); and "An Exact and Perfect Catalogue of All the Plaies that Were Ever Printed," in *The Old Law*, eds. Thomas Middleton, William Rowley and Thomas Heywood (London: Edward Archer, 1656).

[12] Heidi Craig, *Theatre Closure and the Paradoxical Rise of English Renaissance Drama in the Civil Wars* (Cambridge University Press, 2023), esp. 27–32. As Craig demonstrates, the catalogs' inclusiveness and alphabetical order would undermine a commercial function, because they did not showcase better-selling titles, which were instead obscured among lesser-known titles.

[13] Adam G. Hooks, *Selling Shakespeare: Biography, Bibliography, and the Book Trade* (Cambridge University Press, 2016).

bibliographers focused on listing the primary texts of Shakespeare, embedded within comparable lists of titles by Shakespeare's contemporaries.

As it evolved over the course of the century, the professional editorial tradition of the eighteenth century revealed a growing interest in comprehensive enumerative bibliographies of Shakespeare's works. Lewis Theobald's 1733 edition included a "Table of the Several Editions of Shakespeare's Plays, Collected by the Editor," while Edward Capell's 1767 edition of Shakespeare included a "Table of the quartos, folios, ascribed plays, and poems" (1767–8).[14] Although the rise of professional editing around Shakespeare in the eighteenth century is well studied, the implications of the professional editors' creation and inclusion of bibliographies (called "catalogues") within their editions – and enumerative bibliography's broader function as both preliminary and central to the editor's work – have received less attention. Although the full implications of Shakespearean bibliography on eighteenth-century editions of Shakespeare are beyond the scope of this Element, suffice it to say that enumerative bibliography was constitutive of Theobald and Capell's respective editions and was partly how these editors distinguished themselves from their predecessors and professional rivals.[15] For example, Theobald justified the accuracy and assiduity of his editorial labors by pointing to his bibliographical work: the collection, consultation, collation, and cataloging of early copies. As he discusses in his Preface to *The Works of Shakespeare in Seven Volumes* (1733), early copies of Shakespeare plays could be difficult to acquire as they were not necessarily for sale. Theobald explains that Martin Folkes "furnish'd me with the first *folio*

[14] Lewis Theobald, "Table of the Several Editions of Shakespeare's Plays, Collected by the Editor," in *The Works of Shakespeare*, vol. 7 (London: A. Bettesworth *et al.*, 1733), 495–503; and Edward Capell, "Table of his Editions," in *Mr William Shakespeare his Comedies, Histories and Tragedies* (London: J. and R. Tonson, 1767–8), 5 pages [np].

[15] Marcus Walsh, *Shakespeare, Milton and Eighteenth-Century Literary Editing: The Beginnings of Interpretative Scholarship* (Cambridge University Press, 2004). We note, too, that bibliography and listing books is also an important influence on book collecting and many eighteenth- and nineteenth-century editors were likewise collectors, such as Edward Capell and Edmond Malone. Section 2 of this Element touches on the importance of bibliography to collecting and libraries, but a full study is beyond the scope of this volume.

Edition of *Shakespeare*, at a Time when I could not meet with it among the Booksellers; as my obliging Friend *Thomas Coxeter*, Esq; did with several of the old 4^(to) single Plays, which I then had not in my own Collection." Theobald continues that "besides a faithful Collation of all the printed Copies, which I have exhibited in my *Catalogue* of *Editions* at the End of this Work ... I purposely read over *Hall* and *Holingshead*'s Chronicles in the Reigns concern'd; all the Novels in *Italian* ... such Parts of *Plutarch*, from which he had deriv'd any Parts of his *Greek* or *Roman* Story: *Chaucer* and *Spenser*'s Works; all the Plays of *B. Jonson*, *Beaumont* and *Fletcher*, and above 800 old *English* Plays, to ascertain the obsolete and uncommon Phrases in him."[16] By noting the extent of his bibliographical study (enumerated for the reader in the form of a catalog), Theobald was distinguishing himself from his editorial predecessors, especially Alexander Pope. By Theobald's measure, Pope's *Works of Shakespear* (6 volumes, 1725) edited Shakespeare according to the dictates of polite taste of the eighteenth century, rather than textual evidence. Theobald's bibliographically informed corrections of Pope sparked a rivalry and feud, with Pope casting "Tibbald" as a petty pedant in his *Dunciad*.

At the turn of the nineteenth century, the Marquis de Bute's 1805 manuscript bibliography listed not only all editions of Shakespeare's primary texts but also secondary works, described as "all commentaries, etc., regarding that author."[17] The shift from enumerating editions of Shakespeare's works to enumerating Shakespeare *criticism* marks a crucial turning point in Shakespearean enumerative bibliography. Bibliographies by John Britton (1814), John Wilson (1827), William Thomas Lowndes (1831), Thomas Pennant Barton (1834–1836), and James Orchard Halliwell (1841) all attempted, with varying degrees of completeness and accuracy, to create lengthy lists of Shakespeare criticism.[18] The interest in cataloging

---

[16] Theobald, "Preface," in *The Works of Shakespeare*, vol. 1 (London: A. Bettesworth *et al.*, 1733) lxvii–lxviii, emphasis original.

[17] *Catalog written by desire of the Marquis of Bute, and containing, or intended to contain, every edition of Shakespeare, and all commentaries, etc., regarding that author.* 52 pp- [1805], F° G.50.20, Barton Collection, Boston Public Library.

[18] John Britton, *Remarks on the Life and Writing of William Shakespeare: With a List of Essays and Dissertations on his Dramatic Writings* (London: C. Whittingham,

Shakespeare scholarship – already a large, unwieldy, and ever-growing corpus in the early nineteenth century – would ensure that a Shakespeare bibliographer would never run out of work; in the twentieth century, this labor would grow exponentially, partly as Shakespeare's place as a subject of study in the modern university became more secure.

Another landmark of Shakespeare bibliography in English was William Jaggard's *Shakespeare Bibliography: A Dictionary of Every Known Issue of the Writings of Our National Poet and of Recorded Opinion Thereon in the English Language ... With Historical Introduction, Facsimiles, Portraits, and Other Illustrations* (1911) (Figure 2). In his preface, Jaggard (the descendant of the stationers of the First Folio) explained the value of bibliography as "the indispensable tribute to distinguished merit" not only to aid further explorations of a given work or author, but also to pay homage to "literary genius." As Jaggard writes, "In modern days, literary genius asserts its right to a fresh prerogative in the shape of bibliography, a claim no one will grudge. That form of hero-worship honourably serves a double purpose: it fulfills the desire to pay homage where due, and as a key to recorded knowledge, becomes a handmaid to fresh literary labour."[19] Jaggard underscored his own "labour" as bibliographer, noting "the serious nature of this gigantic task" and the millions who have "read and enjoyed" Shakespeare. He dismissed the "pitiful waste of time, breath and ink" devoted to the

1814); John Wilson, *Shaksperiana: Catalogue of all the Books, Pamphlets, etc Relating to Shakespeare* (London: John Wilson, 1827); William Thomas Lowndes, *Shakespeare and his Commentators*, in Lowndes's *Bibliographer's Manual* (London: William Thomas Lowndes, 1831); Thomas Pennant Barton, comp., *Shakespeariana; or, a Complete List of All the Works Relating to Shakespeare* (New York, 1834–1836), 2 volumes, Manuscript. Boston Public Library, MS.f.G.4062.1; James Orchard Halliwell, *Shakesperiana: A Catalogue of the Early Editions of Shakespeare's Plays, and of the Commentaries and Other Publications Illustrative of his Works* (London: John Russell Smith, 1841).

[19] William Jaggard, *Shakespeare Bibliography: A Dictionary of Every Known Issue of the Writings of Our National Poet and of Recorded Opinion Thereon in the English Language ... With Historical Introduction, Facsimiles, Portraits, and Other Illustrations* (Stratford-Upon-Avon: The Shakespeare Press, 1911), v.

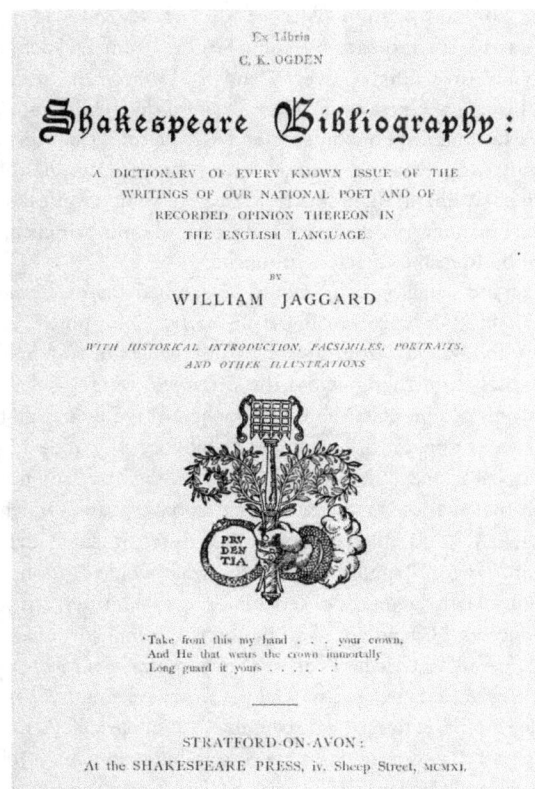

Figure 2 Title page of William Jaggard, *Shakespeare Bibliography* (1911), Internet Archive, https://archive.org/details/shakespearebibli00jagg.

Shakespeare authorship question (perennially a separate section in Shakespearean Bibliography), but noted that even "the cranks [i.e. those who doubt the authorship of Shakespeare] have their uses. They encourage zealots, in the process of holding their own, to study the glorious age of Elizabeth to their infinite pleasure."[20] For several pages, Jaggard quoted paeans to Shakespeare by John Milton, John Dryden, Matthew Arnold, Robert Browning, Oliver Wendell Holmes, and other famous writers and historical figures as a "microcosm of this bibliography." After pages of praise, Jaggard concluded: "and so one might continue, almost without finality, to gyrate, as a moth, round the flashing, dazzling arc of light known as William Shakespeare."[21] While some might dismiss bibliography as perfunctory, designed only to underpin criticism, Jaggard claimed that bibliography itself is criticism.

While Jaggard's bibliography would be scorned for its *lacunae* (as we discuss later), his introduction offered an early, albeit potted, history of Shakespeare bibliography from Meres to his own efforts. Jaggard traced a bibliographical throughline across the centuries, whereby the quest for comprehensiveness represents the bibliographer's "agony and ecstasy." He noted that John Britton, in 1818, compiled "a bibliography of detached essays and dissertations of Shakespeare" and was astonished by the "number and variety of commentaries on the writings of Shakespeare" which "almost exceed credibility."[22] "If that observation fairly represented the student's library a century ago," Jaggard continued, "what would Britton say now!" (Over a century later, Jaggard's observation rings even truer.) In 1827, John Wilson produced a "Catalogue of all the books, pamphlets, etc. relating to Shakespeare." In 1869, Thomas Pennart Barton compiled a 1,000-page manuscript consisting of "a complete list of all the works relating to Shakespeare." Jaggard called attention to the "indispensable" "Bibliographer's manual with its lengthy list of Shakespearana," as well as bibliographies by John Payne Collier and James Orchard Halliwell, the latter producing "exceedingly interesting" lists that were nevertheless "too haphazard."[23] Jaggard's history continued with Shakespeare bibliographers in the late nineteenth century, concluding with the work of Alfred Pollard in 1909.

---

[20] Jaggard, *Shakespeare Bibliography*, vi and vii.
[21] Jaggard, *Shakespeare Bibliography*, xiii.
[22] Jaggard, *Shakespeare Bibliography*, xv.
[23] Jaggard, *Shakespeare Bibliography*, xvi.

After offering this lengthy history of Shakespearean bibliography, Jaggard described the Herculean, nay, Sisyphean, task of the Shakespearean bibliographer:

> one might so continue almost indefinitely, but the titles already exhibited show that a score or more of writers in succession strove to subdue this great toil, but in the main it subdued them, as it nearly did the writer. The tyranny of an exacting profession leaves one little leisure for adventure in bibliography.[24]

As we shall see, this is a sentiment reiterated by the various editors of the *World Shakespeare Bibliography*, lamenting deficits in time, labor, and funds to complete an endless task. Even for the professional Shakespearean, bibliography is often considered subsidiary, despite its foundation to the discipline.[25] Although, like his predecessors, Jaggard aimed at completeness, he acknowledged the invariable shortcomings of his project: "so vast a field can hardly prove to be perfectly gleaned at the first full attempt."[26] He intended to issue "occasional supplements" and asked readers to notify him of any omissions.[27]

Unfortunately for Jaggard, Clark S. Northup did just that the following year, in a very public and lengthy way. In 1912, Northup lamented that "up to the present time no well-trained scholar or group of scholars has undertaken and published an adequate, comprehensive bibliography of the ever-growing literature of Shakespeare."[28] This was not because Northup was unfamiliar with Jaggard. Indeed, Northup reviewed Jaggard's bibliography, along with two others, *Bibliographie. In Jahrbuch der Deutschen Shakespeare Gesellschaft* (1865–1911), and Albert H. Tolman, *Questions on*

---

[24] Jaggard, *Shakespeare Bibliography*, xvii.
[25] Heidi Craig, Laura Estill, and Kris L. May, "A Rationale of Trans-inclusive Bibliography," *Textual Cultures* 16, no. 2 (2023): 1–28, doi.org/10.14434/tc.v16i2.36763.
[26] Jaggard, *Shakespeare Bibliography*, xviii.
[27] Jaggard, *Shakespeare Bibliography*, xviii.
[28] Northup, "On the Bibliography of Shakespeare," 218.

Shakespeare (1910).²⁹ Like Jaggard before him, Northup pressed the necessity of a "full analytical bibliography" of Shakespeare, noting that a good bibliography would prevent the present state of affairs, in which Shakespeare critics go on "repeating themselves or others, ignorant of much that their predecessors have said, each writer playing the game in his own little corner of the universe."³⁰ Unfortunately, Jaggard's was not the "good bibliography" Northup longed for. Even though Jaggard admits that his bibliography is *not* complete, Northup faulted Jaggard's apparent claims of completeness and comprehensiveness, noting that Jaggard "might have said, with becoming modesty, that it was his *aim* to give all these things" rather than, as he does, promise the impossible.³¹ Northup criticized Jaggard for failing to include articles from well-known journals, including *Modern Philology* and *Publications of the Modern Language Association of America*.³² Over the course of several pages, Northup noted relevant articles from those journals overlooked by Jaggard, as well as other important articles. Emphasizing the incompleteness of any bibliography is important because bibliographies can too often be seen as totalizing and complete works. And yet, quibbling over errors devalues the bibliographer's effort, always striving yet invariably incomplete, by focusing on what is not there at the expense of what is.

Northup's review of Jaggard's bibliography, then, amounts to a bibliography itself: judging from other instances where Shakespeare bibliographies begin by listing other bibliographies, we might note the recursiveness of the genre.³³ A key move in twentieth-century Shakespearean bibliography was thus to cite other contemporary Shakespeare bibliographies,

²⁹ For more on German Shakespeare bibliography, see the next section of this Element.
³⁰ Northup, "On the Bibliography of Shakespeare," 218–9.
³¹ Northup, "On the Bibliography of Shakespeare," 219.
³² Northup, "On the Bibliography of Shakespeare," 219.
³³ For instance, "Recent Work in the Shakespearean Field," the bibliography compiled by Albert C. Baugh for 1, no. 1 (1924) of the *SAB* bibliography, lists other bibliographies, including those in Hardin Craig's "Some Problems of Scholarship in the Literature of the Renaissance, Particularly in the English Field" (*Philological Quarterly*, 1, no. 2 [1922]: 81–99), which lists topics in Renaissance literature he thinks are deserving of fuller study, with each topic

exposing the burst of Shakespearean bibliography at the beginning of the twentieth century. The bibliographical efforts of Albert C. Baugh, T. S. Graves, and Hardin Craig in the late 1910s and 1920s indicate that Anglo-American bibliographers of Shakespeare and the English Renaissance took Northup's call to continue Jaggard's work seriously. Nonetheless, the claim (or aspiration) for comprehensiveness would not return until Sidney Thomas's bibliographies for *Shakespeare Quarterly* in the 1950s.

In his critique of Jaggard, Northup noted that "very few book reviews have been entered," a serious omission in his view, since some of the most prominent Shakespeare scholarship has appeared as reviews of other scholarship.[34] Northup complained about the organization and taxonomy of Shakespearean bibliography, as well as deficiencies in organization, labels, categories, and anticipation of its users' needs, especially the difficulty of searching scholarship on individual plays.[35] While lamenting the flaws of Jaggard's bibliography, Northup was pessimistic that anything better would replace it, since "publishers are not eager to risk capital in enterprises of this kind." He continues, "until bibliographical work is more fully appreciated, it is too much to hope that a band of expert bibliographers

---

footnoted with existing scholarship in the area, and T. S. Graves's "Recent Literature [of the English Renaissance]" (*Studies in Philology*, 14, no. 2 [1917]: 218–27), which included a section devoted to Shakespeare (220–23), as well as sections for "Drama," "Spenser," and "Other Writers and Works." The first section of Graves's "Recent Literature of the English Renaissance" (*Studies in Philology*, 20, no. 2 [1923]: 244–92) is devoted to "Bibliographical and General Works" and lists earlier iterations of Baugh and Hardin Craig's bibliographies for *PMLA* and *PQ* respectively; it also lists itself.

[34] For example, Margreta de Grazia and Peter Stallybrass's foundational "The Materiality of the Shakespearean Text" (*Shakespeare Quarterly* 44, no. 3 [1993]: 255–83) could be interpreted as a long-form review of recent work on the two-texts question of *King Lear*.

[35] On the interface of early Shakespeare bibliography and the *WSB*, see Heidi Craig and Laura Estill, "Browse as Interface in Shakesepare's Texts and the World Shakespeare Bibliography Online," in *The Routledge Handbook of Shakespeare and Interface*, eds. Paul Werier and Cliff Budra (Routledge, 2023), 218–233, see esp. 223–24.

shall do the thing over and do it properly."[36] The refrain – or lament? – of bibliographers is consistent: the expense and labor required by comprehensive bibliography does not align with the lack of respect the genre garners. But without it, scholarship would have no solid foundation.

Ultimately, as early attempts to enumerate scholarship about Shakespeare show, bibliographies matter because they are often the first port of call for a researcher. Jaggard's bibliography and its critics demonstrate how bibliography changes what and how we can search. Jaggard's critics show that some early scholars were acutely aware of the need for improved bibliographic practices.

As we trace in the following section, there were two main avenues that bibliographers took to improve bibliographic practices and the currency of the bibliographies thereby produced: with standalone single-volume bibliographies and with periodical bibliographies published repeatedly. The next section begins with German traditions of Shakespearean bibliography in order to illustrate this tension (omnibus bibliographies versus periodical bibliographies), while also pointing to the interrelations between German and Anglo-American bibliography. As we will discuss, this relationship is important for how bibliography was later to develop in England and America. Indeed, *Shakespeare Jahrbuch* was the first to publish a periodical Shakespeare bibliography. As the next section details, German Shakespeare bibliography was used by scholars and collectors in Europe and North America. The German tradition of Shakespeare bibliography is foundational to Shakespeare bibliography writ large, both in the periodical tradition and in the omnibus, single publication tradition.

2 German Traditions of Shakespeare Bibliography: Format, Categories, Meaning

2.1 Cohn's Shakespeare Jahrbuch *Bibliography*

The German tradition of Shakespearean bibliography dates back centuries. It both runs parallel to and is connected to English-language

---

[36] Northup, "On the Bibliography of Shakespeare," 227–28.

bibliographical traditions. The German Shakespeare Society [Deutsche Shakespeare-Gesellschaft] was founded in 1864, and the society's annual journal, the *Shakespeare Jahrbuch*, was first published the following year.[37] *Shakespeare Jahrbuch* is, according to Werner Habicht, "the oldest Shakespeare periodical still existing."[38] With its initial volume, *Shakespeare Jahrbuch* began publishing a "Shakespeare-Bibliographie" by Albert Cohn.

Along with Cohn's "Shakespeare-Bibliographie," two other enumerative sections regularly appeared in *Shakespeare Jahrbuch*: a list of German performances of Shakespeare and a list of the new additions to the German Shakespeare Society's library. The list of performances was compiled by Robert Gericke for its first five years (1876–1880) and continued by Armin Wechsung through the rest of the nineteenth century. Reinhold Köhler, head librarian of the Bibliothek der Deutschen Shakespeare-Gesellschaft, compiled the list of additions to the library from 1868 to 1892, which was later continued by his successors, starting with Paul Friedrich Wilhelm von Bojanowski. Köhler's list showcased the holdings of the German Shakespeare Society library, and the "[Additions to the Library of the German Shakespeare Society]" was so popular that the library periodically published a complete list of holdings in a short booklet separate from the regular publication in the *Jahrbuch* to highlight new acquisitions.[39]

---

[37] Werner Habicht, "Shakespeare and the Founders," *German Shakespeare Studies at the Turn of the Twenty-First Century*, ed. Christa Jansohn (University of Delaware Press, 2006), 239–54, 239.

[38] Habicht, "Shakespeare and the Founders," 426. Facsimiles of early volumes of the *Shakespeare Jahrbuch* are available on HathiTrust; some are also on DigiZeitschriften. For a facsimile of Vol. 1, see catalog.hathitrust.org/Record/000679865. See also the online supplemental material that accompanies this Element for links to additional digitized volumes.

[39] Here and in what follows, square brackets around full quotations indicate that they are translated. The full catalog was published, for instance, in 1871, 1876, 1882, and 1889. Gericke's list of performances (as well as some of his analyses) were sometimes published as "[separately reprinted]" from the *Shakespeare*

Cohn's "Shakespeare-Bibliographie" was published, usually every other year, from the *Jahrbuch*'s first volume in 1865 until volume 36 in 1900, when it was continued by other bibliographers.[40] The bibliography was sorted geographically and then subdivided by topic, a hierarchy of organizing principles that signals the priority of *who* (in terms of national tradition) was undertaking the scholarship over *what* the scholarship was about. The first section featured work from "England und Amerika." Though easily grouped together by Cohn, this combination masked the tension between English and American scholars and bibliographers, as we discuss in the next section. The bulk of the work in the Anglo-American section was published in London and appeared in London-based periodicals such as *Notes and Queries*; both New York and Stratford-upon-Avon appeared multiple times as imprint locations; and some publications indexed were out of Edinburgh, Dublin, and Massachusetts – that is to say, Cohn's focus here was Great Britain and the United States. The second section, about Germany, was followed by France, Holland, and then a category of "[Other Countries]," including Bohemia (present-day Austria), Denmark, Italy, Russia, Sweden, Serbia, and Hungary, each appearing alphabetically. Within each geographical section, Cohn began by listing editions of complete works, individual editions of plays, and then "Shakespeariana," a capacious category that included everything from scholarship about Shakespeare's works to a poem about Shakespeare published in *Notes and Queries*. Cohn specified that the "Shakespeariana" section excluded "[reviews, theater reports, pictorial representations, and musical compositions]."[41] In the German section of the bibliography, but not elsewhere, Cohn included prominent Shakespeare lectures. The German section of the bibliography is 70 percent of the length of the section from

Jahrbuch. Köhler's complete catalog, however, was published without mention of the *Jahrbuch*.

[40] For the first six years, Cohn's bibliography was published annually with the exception of Vol. 4. From then on, the bibliography was published biennially with a couple of triennial exceptions (Vol. 27, 1892; Vol. 33, 1897).

[41] Albert Cohn, "Shakespeare-Bibliographie 1864, und 1865 Januar bis Juli," *Shakespeare Jahrbuch* 1 (1865): 418–47, 433.

"England und Amerika."[42] The overall effect of this bibliography is to demonstrate Germany's excellence in Shakespeare scholarship and to flag the importance of German Shakespeare scholarship on the global stage.

Because Cohn's bibliographies were reprinted separately from the *Jahrbuch*, they achieved circulation to many parts of the world.[43] One such copy of the reprinted bibliography, now at the University of Michigan, includes a letter Cohn sent with a copy of his bibliography, likely to Joseph Crosby (Figure 3).[44] Crosby, a nineteenth-century Shakespearean, owned "one of the best" private Shakespeare libraries in America.[45] Writing to Crosby, Cohn recounted how "Mr Hubbard of Boston has sent me part II of his catalogue" – that is, James Mascarene Hubbard sent the second part of his own *Catalogue of the Works of William Shakespeare, Original and Translated, Together with the Shakespeariana Embraced in the Barton Collection of the Boston Public Library* (1880). Cohn praised Hubbard's *Catalogue* as "really admirable for accuracy" with "a wonderfully lucid arrangement," adding, "I think it is by far the best Shakespearian bibliogr. we possess, though being a catalogue of one particular collection only." Here, Cohn blurred the line between catalog (holdings of a given library) and bibliography (list of materials available not restricted to a given site or owner), a line that had been clearly demarcated in the *Jahrbuch* publications: Köhler published the catalog of the German Shakespeare Society Library, and Cohn published the bibliography of as many pieces of scholarship as

---

[42] The breakdown is as follows: "England und Amerika," pp. 418-top of 432; "Deutschland," pp. 432-top of 442; "Frankreich," pp. 442–43; "Holland" pp. 444-top of 446; and "Verschiedene Länder" pp. 447–48, including Bohemia (present-day Austria), Denmark, Italy, Russia, Sweden, Serbia, and Hungary (alphabetical in German).

[43] At the time of writing (2026), WorldCat lists libraries with holdings of Cohn's bibliographies in Europe, North America, and Australia.

[44] Cohn, "Shakespeare-Bibliographie." Sammelband gathering bibliographies from 1871–1878, PR 2885.A1 C67 1871, University of Michigan Special Collections, catalog.hathitrust.org/Record/004207944.

[45] John W. Velz, "Joseph Crosby and the Shakespeare Scholarship of the Nineteenth Century," *Shakespeare Quarterly* 27, no. 3 (1976): 316–28, 316.

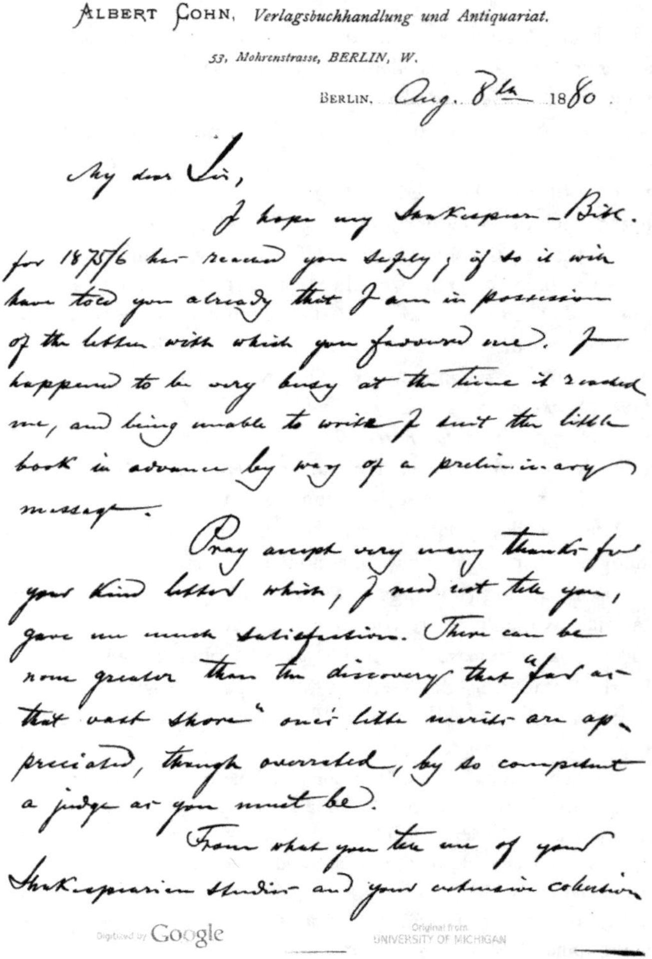

ALBERT COHN, *Verlagsbuchhandlung und Antiquariat.*

53, Mohrenstrasse, BERLIN, W.

BERLIN, Aug. 8th 1880.

My dear Sir,

I hope my Shakespear-Bibl. for 1875/6 has reached you safely; if so it will have told you already that I am in possession of the letter with which you favoured me. I happened to be very busy at the time it reached me, and being unable to write I sent the little book in advance by way of a preliminary message.

Pray accept very many thanks for your kind letters which, I need not tell you, gave me much satisfaction. There can be none greater than the discovery that "far as that vast shore" one's little merits are appreciated, though overrated, by so competent a judge as you must be.

From what you tell me of your Shakespearian studies and your extensive collection

Figure 3 Opening of Cohn's letter to Crosby, included with the 1872 reprint of Cohn's bibliography. University of Michigan Library (Special Collections Research Center). Available: https://catalog.hathitrust.org/Record/004207944.

he could find, regardless of where they were housed. For Cohn, both kinds of enumerative work (cataloging and bibliography) were valuable, and both needed to be disseminated widely because they were foundational to scholarship.

Based in Berlin, Cohn was in active correspondence with Shakespeare scholars and book collectors in America and England. Given the ambitious scope of Cohn's bibliography, it is not surprising that he repeated the perennial request of bibliographers in his note to Crosby:

> Whenever you come across any Shakespearian articles in periodicals or newspapers, I will sincerely thank you to send me a note of them, if you cannot send the papers themselves, for which I would gladly pay. It is by 'united strength' only that bibliographical works can be made useful.[46]

Cohn wrote that other prominent English and American Shakespeareans of the day, including Samuel Timmins (a businessman who was one of the founders of the Birmingham Shakespeare Library, United Kingdom) and Horace Howard Furness (one of the foremost editors of Shakespeare, based in Philadelphia) already sent him materials, but acknowledged that despite this existing correspondence, "at present most of the American things are escaping me."[47]

In his letter, Cohn apologized to Crosby that the material he had enumerated only covered a sliver of Shakespearean bibliography – in this case, from April 1872 to the end of 1873, as the title page announces. As a bibliography published in a periodical, this was to be expected: it updated previous bibliographies from the *Jahrbuch* and was

---

[46] Cohn, letter bound with "Shakespeare-Bibliographie." Sammelband gathering bibliographies from 1871–1878, PR 2885.A1 C67 1871, University of Michigan Special Collections, catalog.hathitrust.org/Record/004207944.

[47] Stephen Roberts, "Timmins, Samuel (1826–1902)," *Oxford Dictionary of National Biography* (2013), doi.org/10.1093/ref:odnb/104869; and Felix E. Schelling, "A Memorial of Horace Howard Furness," *Shakespeare Biography and Other Papers, Chiefly Elizabethan* (University of Pennsylvania Press, 1937), 71–84.

meant to be used in conjunction with those previous bibliographies. Without access to past issues of the *Jahrbuch* (or all past copies of the standalone reprints), however, the bibliography would have been woefully inadequate in giving a full picture of the field. Furthermore, the bibliographer building on existing bibliographies would have had to remember or reference what had already been indexed. Cohn lamented his busyness:

> otherwise I should have put together long ago the vastness of materials I have collected for a complete Shakespeare-Bibliography which, if the plan could be carried out such as I have conceived it, would not, I believe, be altogether unwelcome to students, in spite of all that has been done already in the same direction. For the present I must content myself by giving a specimen of it in the next 'Jahrbuch' independent of the bibliography for 1879/80.

Cohn never realized his best-laid plans for a standalone bibliography as the culmination of his work.

Given that Cohn himself never published an omnibus version of his bibliography, it is unsurprising that readers and librarians gathered his work together in sammelbände, that is, bespoke user-created volumes. The University of California Library, for instance, includes one sammelband that brings together six volumes of Cohn's reprinted bibliography, functionally creating one volume spanning 1881–1893.[48] Although sammelbände like these gathered together multiple bibliographies, they still did not offer a unified access point, as Cohn's imagined omnibus bibliography would. That is to say, a researcher would have to search the same section across multiple volumes instead of looking for a single heading that combined the material from the six previous volumes. (Cohn's decision to organize his bibliography by geography first would also not have lent itself to finding all

---

[48] The facsimile of this volume is available at HathiTrust: catalog.hathitrust.org/Record/100794235.

relevant material on a given topic because researchers had to search in multiple sections.)

Justin Winsor, librarian of Harvard University from 1877 and first president of the American Library Association, also gathered Cohn's bibliographies into a bespoke sammelband (Figure 4a). Winsor prefaced the collection with this note: "The volume contains some bibliographical data, memoranda, scraps etc gathered by me for private use" (Figure 4b). Winsor's "use" of these collected papers (mostly printed, with some handwritten letters) is clear from their organization: his first handwritten section titles are "First Folio Prices" and "First Folio Reprints"; in short, he compiled these pages from sale catalogs, advertisements, and handwritten notes because of his interest in Shakespeare bibliography and book collecting. Winsor published his own *Bibliography of the Original Quartos and Folios of Shakespeare, with Particular Reference to Copies in America* in 1876 and "Shakespeare's Poems: A Bibliography of the Earlier Editions" in 1878. Winsor's sammelband, which included Cohn's 1877–78 bibliography, was likely gathered as part of his research process, but also continued to grow after Winsor published his *Bibliography*. In his bespoke volume, Winsor inserts a dedicated title page at the start of the *Jahrbuch* bibliography, which reads, "Cohn's Bibliography, 1877–78." Winsor gathered Cohn's bibliography with sale catalogs and other bibliographies, including "A List of the Editions of Shakespeare's Works Published in America" (published by the Shakespeare Memorial Library, 1889). Whether consciously or not, Winsor followed Cohn's organizational system with his handwritten section title pages: "English and American catalogues" followed by "German catalogues." Under the title "German catalogues," Winsor collected prominent book sales in Germany, including the sale of the collection belonging to Robert Gericke, who inaugurated the list of German performances in *Shakespeare Jahrbuch* and whose books were sold after his death in 1880. For both Cohn and Winsor, the periodical publication of bibliographies was only the start of scholarship: these cumulative reference works had to be gathered by the researcher and put in conversation with other resources.

Cohn's planned (but never realized) omnibus bibliography and the user-created sammelbände in which we find his work highlight some of the challenges of periodical bibliographies for scholars, especially the need to

Figure 4a Justin Winsor's Handwritten title page: "Shakespearian Bibliography" Source: https://catalog.hathitrust.org/Record/102669630 (image 5). Widener Library, Harvard University, 12455.68.

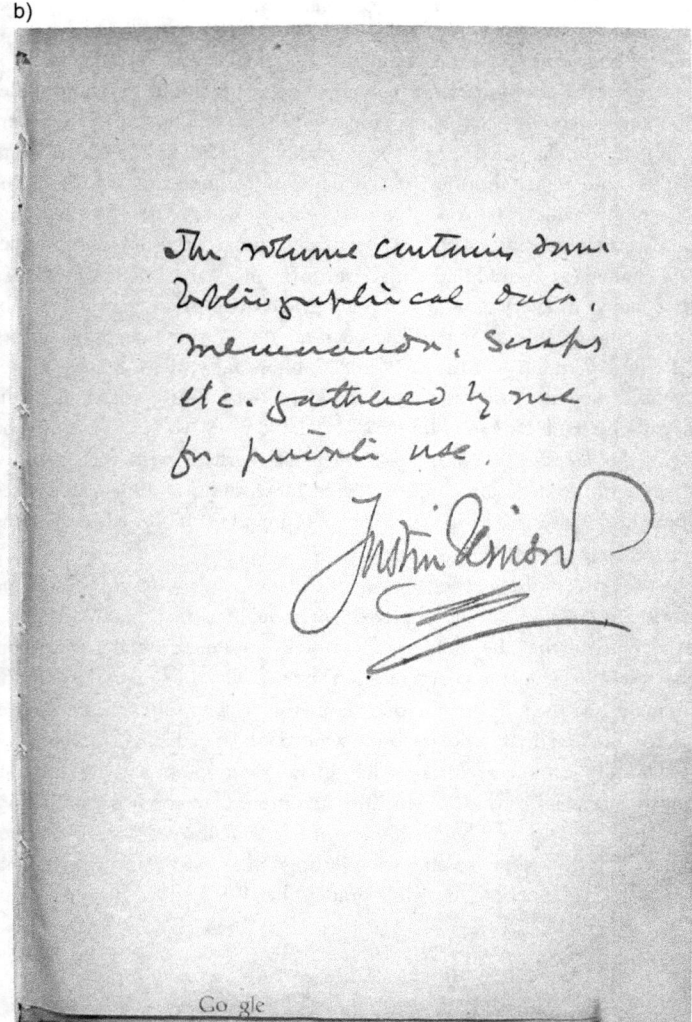

Figure 4b Winsor's prefatory note. Source: https://catalog.hathitrust.org/Record/102669630 (image 7). Widener Library, Harvard University, 12455.68.

locate multiple issues of the bibliography and then repeat the same topic or keyword search in volume after volume. And yet periodical bibliographies were in high demand because they included recent scholarship. Subscribers to the *Jahrbuch* clamored for the bibliography, leaving editor Karl Elze to add this note to the bottom of the table of contents in Vol. 9: "[The bibliography, which Mr. A. Cohn was regrettably prevented from editing, will be in the next yearbook]."[49] Logistically, too, periodical bibliographies create challenges around updating past omissions. After his first published bibliography, in every subsequent bibliography, Cohn noted that his publication included additions that had been missing in previous publications. By the time he published the 1881–1882 bibliography, the title page notice advertised the scale of these backwards insertions: "[With additions to the bibliography from 1864 in volumes I, II, III, V, VI, VIII, X, XII, XIV, and XVI of the *Jahrbuch*]."[50] Perhaps with pride, perhaps with weariness, or perhaps with both, Cohn carefully listed these additions, specifying each volume in which the overlooked (but now included) pieces of scholarship were meant to appear.

In 1900, Richard Schröder took over the monumental task of compiling *Shakespeare Jahrbuch*'s bibliography on an annual basis. In his first preface, Schröder noted that the bibliography would continue regular publication, with some improvements to organization and usability, including the addition of an index and the introduction of a numbering system for entries. Schröder took for granted that scholars both wanted and needed a "[precise and systematically organized Shakespeare bibliography]," saying, "[Opinions about the necessity of this do not differ any more than about the difficulties of such a huge task]."[51] The *Shakespeare Jahrbuch* bibliography continued for another eight decades, even appearing during both world wars, until its final appearance, the "Shakespeare-Bibliography für 1979," edited by Karl-Heinz

---

[49] Karl Elze, editor, *Shakespeare Jahrbuch* 9 (1874): IV.

[50] Cohn, "Shakespeare Bibliographie 1881 und 1882," separately printed from *Shakespeare Jahrbuch* XVIII ([1883]): 1.

[51] Schröder, "Shakespeare-Bibliographie 1900," *Shakespeare Jahrbuch* 37 (1901), 315.

Magister.[52] While periodical bibliography was not the ideal system, it did offer some benefits, including timeliness and the ability to offer corrections. Cohn's ongoing bibliography indeed offered users information about recently published works. When Northup wrote his evaluation "On the Bibliography of Shakespeare" in 1912, he praised *Shakespeare Jahrbuch*'s bibliography, noting that from 1900 to 1912 there were over six thousand items cataloged in the bibliography by Schröder, Gustav Becker, and Hans Daffis. Northup framed these bibliographies as a nationalist endeavor where Germans outpaced the Anglo-American bibliographers who we discussed in the previous section: "German scholars, excelling in many fields, may also point with pride to this series. As for Shakespearean Bibliography in England and America, after 300 years, we now have – Mr. Jaggard!"[53] Northup's derisive exclamation underscores his low opinion of Jaggard's bibliography.

2.2 Early Standalone German Bibliographies

In 1865, the same year Cohn launched the *Shakespeare Jahrbuch* bibliography, Franz Thimm published the first edition of his bibliography, *Shakespeariana from 1564 to 1864*.[54] Thimm, a German bibliographer living in London, focused his work on English, German, and French publications. Thimm positioned himself as the successor to previous (flawed) bibliographies, beginning his preface with the bald statement: "The first 'Shakespeariana,' by Wilson, published in 1827, was too imperfect to be of much use."[55] Thimm continued, weighing the pros and cons of various other bibliographies in English, Dutch, and German, including Halliwell's (1841), one by Jurriaan Moulin (Holland, 1845), and an anonymous 1852 bibliography of German Shakespeare studies. Thimm praises P. H. Sillig's *Die Shakespeare-Literature bis Mitte 1854* (1855) as "the most perfect production of its kind."[56] With its extensive content and handsome index, Sillig's bibliography would indeed have been more usable than others at the

---

[52] *Shakespeare Jahrbuch* 117 (1981).
[53] Northup, "On the Bibliography of Shakespeare," 229.
[54] Franz Thimm, *Shakspeariana from 1564 to 1864. An Account of the Shakesperian Literature of England, Germany and France during Three Centuries* (London, 1865).
[55] Thimm, *Shakspeariana*, v. [56] Thimm, *Shakspeariana*, v.

time. Thimm's introduction demonstrates what scholars wanted from a bibliography: comprehensiveness and usability.

In his first edition, Thimm bragged that his own contribution had "over 600 more [entries] than Sillig."[57] And yet, unsurprisingly, Thimm's edition also had numerous gaps; he expanded his publication by 50 percent for the second edition in 1872, which he termed a "supplement." In his preface to the second edition, Thimm offered specific instructions on how to incorporate the new publication into the old (hoping that folks had not yet bound their bibliographies either separately or with other works): "The Supplement has been printed with the view of incorporating it with the first edition, so that the English part should be bound up after page 48; the German part after page 81; and the French part should be canceled altogether, and the new sheets inserted instead."[58] In short, standalone bibliographies could not add new content without encouraging their readers to literally take apart their books.

Other standalone bibliographies, such as Ludwig Unflad's *Die Shakespeare-literatur in Deutschland* [*Shakespeare Literature in Germany*] (1880), were useful but often never updated. Unflad's preface emphasized his work's "[practical use]"; and though he offered the traditional call for people to contact him with things he had missed so that he could create "[a supplement or possible new edition]," it seems that no supplement ever appeared.[59] Unflad's subtitle and preface underscored that his bibliography was only an attempt and would necessarily be incomplete: "[The greatest care was taken in collecting the material for this little book, although I make no claim to completeness; it is but an attempt.]"[60] Whether published in periodicals, as a single volume, or now online, Shakespearean bibliography is, as Schröder stated, "[a huge task.]"

The main problem with one-and-done bibliographies is thus readily apparent. Publications about Shakespeare did not stop in 1855 or 1865 or 1880; any bibliography published as a book would be incomplete before it even reached the hands of readers.

---

[57] Thimm, *Shakspeariana*, v. [58] Thimm, *Shakspeariana* (1872, 2nd ed.), [iii].

[59] Ludwig Unflad, *Die Shakespeare-literatur in Deutschland* (Munich, 1880), [ii].

[60] Unflad, *Die Shakespeare-literatur*, [ii].

2.3 Ebisch and Schücking's A Shakespeare Bibliography

One of the most impressive and influential German bibliographies was Walther Ebisch and Levin L. Schücking's *A Shakespeare Bibliography*, which was published in 1931 and covered the years up until 1929. This was an English-language bibliography by a German librarian-scholar duo. As the title page of the volume announces, Ebisch was "Librarian of the English Seminar" at the University of Leipzig, and Schücking was a professor at the University of Leipzig when this volume appeared. Its publication by Oxford University Press demonstrates that it was intended for a widespread English-speaking audience.

Ebisch and Schücking's bibliography drew heavily on German Shakespeare studies and therefore emphasized German scholarship. In the section of "Translations of Shakespeare," Ebisch and Schücking begin with "German Translations," the only language area to receive subdivisions ("General Works dealing with German Translators" and "The most important German Translations"); this is followed by "Other Germanic Languages," a short section which lists only three translations: Carl August Hagberg's "monumental" (to use Ebisch and Schücking's adjective) Swedish translations; Valdemar Osterberg's Danish translations and commentary; and Finnur Jónsson's list of Icelandic translations.[61] "Romance languages" (subdivided into "French" and "Spanish and Portuguese") and "Slavonic Translations" share a single page, compared to the four pages devoted to only the most "important" German translations. Similar emphasis on German Shakespeare scholarship is evident in the rest of the section on Shakespeare's influence. Despite the prevalence of German content in the bibliography, Lawrence Marsden Price laments that even though "the *Shakespeare Bibliography* had its origins in a German university," Ebisch and Schücking misconstrue "elementary facts regarding the history of Shakespeare in Germany."[62] Price points out key missing German translations, scholars,

---

[61] Walther Ebisch and Levin L. Schücking, *A Shakespeare Bibliography* (Oxford University Press, 1931), 162.

[62] Lawrence Marsden Price, review of *A Shakespeare Bibliography*, by Walther Ebisch and Levin L. Schücking, *The Journal of English and Germanic Philology* 31, no. 1 (1932): 150–52, 152.

and apparent confusion of people, adding: "one would expect the part dealing with that subject [the history of Shakespeare in Germany] to be one of the soundest portions of the book, but one is led by the evidence to hope that it is the worst."[63] Despite the errors, Price notes that Ebisch and Schücking's bibliography positions German scholarship as apace with Anglo-American Shakespeare scholarship in terms of volume of entries and organization.

However lopsided their results were, Ebisch and Schücking at least attempted truly global coverage. As they noted in their preface,

> The reason why this task [a global Shakespeare bibliography] has nevertheless up till now not been taken in hand consists in the almost inexhaustible riches of Shakespearian literature. It is a subject to which every new year brings new material. To register all of it would be neither desirable nor indeed possible. In other words, the task entails the danger of *selection*.[64]

Although Ebisch and Schücking's bibliography acknowledged that comprehensiveness was not possible, they did actively redress some gaps. In 1937, they released a 97-page *Supplement for the Years 1930–1935 to A Shakespeare Bibliography*. They explained the rationale, organization, and scope of the volume in their preface to the *Supplement*:

> Since the *Shakespeare Bibliography* was published in 1931, so many contributions to Shakespearian study have appeared in print that the necessity of a supplement to our former work makes itself felt. The subsequent pages follow the method and arrangement of the main work. They contain the new publications from 1930 to April 1936; furthermore, the opportunity has been taken to repair a few important omissions in the original work.[65]

---

[63] Price, review, 152.
[64] Ebisch and Schücking, *A Shakespeare Bibliography*, [v], emphasis original.
[65] Ebisch and Schücking, *Supplement for the Years 1930–1935 to A Shakespeare Bibliography* (Oxford University Press, 1936), [ii].

The bibliographers concluded with the same outreach familiar to scholars today, saying they "would be grateful for any suggestions brought forward to fill in the gaps or to improve the work done."[66] Both the original *Bibliography* and its supplement were later reissued in 1968 by Benjamin Blom, a New York publisher. Even decades out of date with current scholarship, this book was valuable enough to merit a reprint. For G. Blakemore Evans, writing in the 1960s, Ebisch and Schücking's volume was "the old standard."[67]

No bibliographer works in a vacuum. Ebisch and Schücking lived and worked in Germany through both world wars. Schücking was a pacifist, serving as chair of the Silesian branch of the German Peace Society from 1918 to 1923.[68] In 1933, he "was threatened with dismissal" from his professorship at Leipzig University because of his pacifist views. That same year, however, he was a signatory on the 1933 "[Vow of Allegiance of the Professors of the German Universities and High-Schools to Adolf Hitler and the National Socialistic State]," wherein German professors proclaimed their support of Hitler and the Nazis. (Ebisch, as a librarian, was likely not even asked to sign.) Schücking continued to be persecuted for his pacifist beliefs, eventually losing his salary in 1942. The English Wikipedia page for Schücking notes that he recanted his pro-Hitler beliefs, but currently offers no citations; he seems to have been consistently pacifist despite signing the "Vow."[69]

It is hardly a surprise that Ebisch and Schücking did not publish additional supplements to their 1937 bibliography, as political tensions escalated and war was officially declared in 1939. Decades after the war, in 1963, Gordon Ross Smith published *A Classified Shakespeare Bibliography, 1936–1958*, which he positioned as a successor to Ebisch and Schücking's *Bibliography* and *Supplement*. With permission from

---

[66] Ebisch and Schucking, *Supplement*, [ii].

[67] G. Blakemore Evans, review of *A Classified Shakespeare Bibliography, 1936–1958*, by Gordon Ross Smith, *The Journal of English and Germanic Philology* 63, no. 1 (1964): 165–66, 165.

[68] Haenicke Gunta, "Schücking, Levin Ludwig" *Neue Deutsche Biographie* 23 (2007), www.deutsche-biographie.de/pnd117124931.html.

[69] "Levin Ludwig Schücking," wikipedia.org/wiki/Levin_Ludwig_Sch%C3%BCcking (accessed August 2025).

Schücking, he continued using their organizational system. Maintaining the organizational system would make it easier for users to use this reference work in concert with the others. Smith's *Classified Bibliography* more than doubled Ebisch and Schücking's content. Although Smith was a professor at The Pennsylvania State University, his contribution bears consideration in this section because it continues the tradition started by Ebisch and Schücking. At Penn State, Smith worked with Harrison T. Meserole, who would (a decade later, in 1976) go on to become editor of the *World Shakespeare Bibliography*. (We discuss Meserole's work at more length in Section 5.) Although this section focuses on German bibliography, efforts by Thimm, Ebisch and Schücking, and Smith demonstrate that attempts to classify national contributions to bibliography show how bibliography and scholarship often traverse borders.

As R. W. Dent notes in a footnote to his review of Smith's *Classified Shakespeare Bibliography*, Smith emphasizes German reception and production of Shakespeare, like, we add, Ebisch and Schücking. Dent extends the caveat: "the user of Smith should be aware that sections on productions in foreign countries other than Germany, or on translations other than those in German, are thoroughly unreliable guides."[70] As the next section details, at this time (1959–1964), Dent was editing the annual bibliography of Shakespeare research that appeared in *Shakespeare Quarterly*, making him particularly aware of Smith's omissions and strengths. Dent attributed the uneven coverage to "the correspondents of the bibliographies [Smith] has employed."[71] We see this unevenness continue to this day with purportedly global Shakespeare bibliographies that are only as good as their locally situated contributor network. Even as information appears increasingly online, for example, it is often through the contributions of individual correspondents that the *World Shakespeare Bibliography*, for instance, is able to include the geographic range of coverage it does.

It is not simply what we include in a bibliography that makes it useful: it is how we can navigate and find that information. Dent's extensive ten-page

---

[70] R. W. Dent, "A Test for 'Accomplished Scholars,'" *Shakespeare Quarterly* 16, no. 2 (1965): 247–55, 248.

[71] Dent, "A Test," 248.

review of Smith's *Classified Shakespeare Bibliography* recognized the labor that went into this bibliography while also noting its omissions and the challenges a "user" (to echo Dent's phrase) faces when searching for material in a categorized bibliography (i.e., "*Classified*" into different topical category headings), particularly when it comes to finding materials that could be placed under multiple headings. Smith's bibliography included limited (but not necessarily intuitive) cross-referencing, as Dent notes with multiple examples included in his review. The challenges of finding materials are further exacerbated when it comes to non-English content. As Dent points out, "Obviously, attempting to place so huge a body of material within so complexly classified a bibliography posed difficulties too great for any one man, probably too great even for a group of experts in the various subject matters."[72] S. F. Johnson notes, "Principles of classification are inconsistent where they are not fuzzy."[73] Smith himself acknowledged the challenges of categorizing scholarship at this scale: "An unavoidable problem with a classified bibliography of this size is that there are either a great multiplicity of classes or else classes of such size that they cease to be classes."[74]

Indeed, the challenges for use (especially navigability) are among the largest complaints reviewers of Smith's volume noted. Herbert Howarth devoted almost a full page in his review to explaining the challenges of finding materials on a given topic for a research paper, asking, "Where must I look amid his 784 pages?"[75] Johnson projects confusion onto an imagined student user: "Apparently part of the putative audience of this book is the busy graduate student. Our students, however, are not readily going to find what we should like them readily to find in this reference work."[76] While usually opening with praise of this volume's contents,

---

[72] Dent, "A Test," 250.

[73] S. F. Johnson, review of *A Classified Shakespeare Bibliography: 1936–1958*, *Renaissance News* 17, no. 1 (1964): 4–8, 7.

[74] Gordon Ross Smith, *A Classified Shakespeare Bibliography, 1936–1958* (Pennsylvania State University Press, 1963), xlix.

[75] Herbert Howarth, "A Guide for Scholars," *The Journal of General Education* 16, no. 1 (1964): 72–74, 73.

[76] Johnson, review, 6.

scholars suggest that the contents are much less usable because they are not easily navigable due to the lack of clearly defined and evenly applied classifications and cross-references.

Smith explained that he added new categories to Ebisch and Schücking's classification system as needed, because, as he noted, "that bibliography contains only about 3,800 items, and this one over 20,000."[77] Smith's thirty-five-page table of contents for the bibliography has multiple broad categories, such as "Shakespeare's Life," and "Shakespeare's Sources, Literary Influences, and Cultural Relations." Each category is divided into multiple subcategories, and then further subdivided: for instance, "Shakespeare's Stage and the Production of His Plays" has two subcategories, "The Theatre," and "The Actors and their Art." "The Theatre" is broken down into three smaller categories: "History of the Elizabethan Theatre," "The Court and the Stage," and "Public and Private Theatres." "History of Elizabethan Theatre" has three additional subheadings: "Sources," "General Treatises," and "Puritan Attack upon the Stage." While the latter two of these sub(-sub-sub-)headings are not divided, "Sources" is divided with even more nuance into topics such as "The Revels at Court," "Philip Henslowe," and "Sources, Other," the last of which has yet another layer of classification to itemize its contents, including "The Keeling Journal," "The Manningham Diary," and simply "Other." These classifications follow, by and large, Ebisch and Schücking, though Smith eschewed using the Greek alphabet for his sub-subclassifications. Compare, for instance, Ebisch and Schücking's "XII. SHAKESPEARE'S INFLUENCE THROUGH THE CENTURIES > 2. Shakespeare's Influence Outside England > c. The Latin Countries > α. France > bb. Influence on Individual Writers" to Smith's "XIII. SHAKESPEARE'S INFLUENCE THROUGH THE CENTURIES > 3. Shakespeare's Influence Outside England > c. The Latin Countries > (1) France > (b) Influence on Individual French Writers > iv. Stendhal." Smith added a subcategory naming individual authors (because they are not to be found in an index); his added categories (such as the "XII. COMPARISONS WITH OTHER WRITERS") change the numbering system, but the organizational principles are similar. These

---

[77] Smith, *A Classified Shakespeare Bibliography*, xlix.

complicated nested headings (offering a taxonomy in its truest sense) were simultaneously necessary for information retrieval and challenging for users.

While classifications are often what make a bibliography useful, they can also stymy discovery. No two people, be they bibliographers or information seekers, will necessarily classify the same article in the same way, even if given the same taxonomy to work with. Previously, classifications used to be the foundational way to navigate longer bibliographies and scholarly materials. With Smith's *Bibliography*, the classification was the *only* way to navigate, particularly without an index. Today, with various search functions in digital databases and bibliographies, users typically do not turn to the classifications in the same way; yet clearly defined classifications still structure the data (and its findability and navigability), even if those classifications sometimes now operate behind the scenes. Classifying and cross-referencing material adequately takes subject expertise, thought, and planning.

Here is an example of how researchers could be hindered rather than helped by these classifications, as Howarth noted in his review. If a researcher wanted to find information about *Arden of Faversham*, it would make sense to turn to the eponymous subcategory in the "Apocrypha" section, where they would find entries C290–C307. This would omit, however, three French translations of *Arden of Faversham* (by André Montaigne, B651a; by André Gide, B683; and by Laurette Brunius and Loleh Bellon, B729), none of which appear in the same subsection of the translation section, because these are sorted by translator and not work. Given that Félix Carrère's translation of *Arden of Faversham* appears in the "Apocrypha" section twice (C301, his thesis; and C301a, its publication), a researcher might not realize that there are additional translations in an entirely different section. Carrère's published translation also appears in "translations" with a different reference number (B671), but his thesis does not. As this example from a less-popular play shows, navigating the classification system was cumbersome and could lead to missing the very material the bibliography was designed to surface. These problems are multiplied with canonical and popular works, which are more likely to be written about as comparators, more likely to be translated, and more likely to appear in multiple categories (such as those relating to performance and recordings).

Though Smith's bibliography owed much to Ebisch and Schücking, particularly concerning its classifications, it was far more expansive. R. C. Bald extols "Ebisch and Schücking's" as a "selective bibliography," noting that "part of its value lay in the skill with which the selection was made."[78] Smith's foreword explains the scope of his volume and pushes back against ideas of objective selectivity with its opening line: "The best argument for so comprehensive a bibliography as this is that no two judgments are alike, that one does not and should not rely on the infallibility of a single source, and therefore that any user of a selective bibliography is likely to be haunted by the fear and perhaps the likelihood that something particularly relevant to his study has been missed."[79] For Evans, Ebisch and Schücking's *Shakespeare Bibliography* was, on the one hand "misleadingly selective"; on the other hand, he found the sheer amount of material covered in Smith's bibliography "sobering."[80] Ebisch and Schücking's work had 3,800 entries in the first volume. By Evans's count, Smith's bibliography includes "around 20,000 books, articles, notes, etc. on Shakespeare and subjects related to Shakespeare in a little over twenty years, and Professor Smith suggests a possible tripling of this number by the end of the century!"[81] It is, as Evans describes, a "Babylonian pile" of scholarship to be waded through or added to.[82]

As he himself described it, Smith's bibliography is not a "comprehensive bibliography."[83] It is, rather, an omnibus: it gathers together materials from existing bibliographies. Smith lists all of his bibliographic sources, beginning with the annual *Shakespeare Quarterly* bibliography, because it provided the most fodder for his bibliography. Other sources Smith gathered into his bibliography include review-articles such as those in *Year's Work in*

---

[78] R. C. Bald, review of *A Classified Shakespeare Bibliography, 1936–58*, by Gordon Ross Smith, *Modern Philology* 62, no. 1 (1964): 68–69, 69.

[79] Smith, *A Classified Shakespeare Bibliography*, xlv. [80] Evans, review, 165.

[81] Evans, review, 165. According to the *WSB* entry, Smith's *Bibliography* includes 20,527 entries.

[82] Evans, review, 165. [83] Smith, *A Classified Shakespeare Bibliography*, xlv.

English Studies, the *Shakespeare Jahrbuch* bibliography, and the *Shakespeare Association Bulletin* bibliography, as well as *Dissertation Abstracts International* (the analog precursor to ProQuest's *Digital Dissertations*). The workflow of searching existing bibliographies and databases resonates still today – indeed, it is one of the practices still used to update the online *World Shakespeare Bibliography*.

The desire to create an omnibus bibliography that brings together existing Shakespeare bibliographies is both understandable and laudable. Smith writes: "My purpose has been to provide a bibliography that scholars and students might use with the confidence that they would not also have to consult the bibliographies from which this one has been compiled."[84] Howarth emphasizes this in the conclusion of his review: "In fact, what Dr. Smith claims for his bibliography is that scholars and students may now find in one volume the material for which they would hitherto have had to search through forty and more. He has placed the academic world in his debt."[85] Yet, despite such lofty goals and praise, Smith points out that his *Bibliography* is still not the starting and ending point for research. Smith suggests "that the student should not rely on this bibliography alone."[86] Smith notes the importance of looking to Ebisch and Schücking for earlier scholarship, gives concrete suggestions on how to supplement their work by turning to other bibliographies compiled before 1936, and points out that for scholarship past 1958 researchers will need to continue to consult multiple sources. While Smith's impressive bibliography did streamline some of the labor of finding information for researchers, it was not intended to be a one-stop shop.

The bibliographies surveyed in this section, from Cohn's recurring contribution to the *Shakespeare Jahrbuch* to Smith's *Bibliography* highlight one of the key themes from this Element: the format of bibliographies underpins how they are able to offer information. On the one hand, periodical bibliographies offer up-to-date information, but, before the pre-digital era, required a researcher to access and search multiple volumes. On

---

[84] Smith, *A Classified Shakespeare Bibliography*, xlv.
[85] Howarth, "Guide for Scholars," 74.
[86] Smith, *A Classified Shakespeare Bibliography*, li.

the other hand, single-volume bibliographies could be a one-time purchase but quickly fall out of date. As this section has traced, early German bibliographies have both direct influences (to readers and users, such as Winsor, and to other bibliographers, such as Smith) as well as general influences because of their categorizations and comprehensiveness. Bibliographies are shaped by the people who work on them and their access to information. While bibliographies seem to impart neutral information, they are shaped by principles of inclusion and exclusion, as well as by how their information is categorized.

3 *Shakespeare Association Bulletin* and *Shakespeare Quarterly*: Anglo-American Annual Shakespeare Bibliographies

The first iteration of the *World Shakespeare Bibliography* appeared in *Shakespeare Quarterly* in 1950. But the *WSB* was preceded by an earlier bibliography (in a journal that was a predecessor to *SQ*), which in turn was preceded by various efforts to enumerate work on and by Shakespeare. This section focuses on twentieth-century enumerative bibliographies of Shakespeare criticism. While the emphasis is on Anglo-American bibliographies, nation- and language-specific bibliographies were in constant dialogue with one another, as the previous section has shown.

3.1 The Shakespeare Association Bulletin *Bibliography, 1924–1948*

The precursor to *SQ* was the *Shakespeare Association Bulletin* (*SAB*), first published in June 1924 by the newly formed Shakespeare Association of America (SAA). The first issue included "Recent Work in the Shakespearean Field" compiled by Professor Albert C. Baugh and listing titles of new scholarship on Shakespeare. From the beginning, the *SAB* and this bibliography were self-conscious about the necessity of both a Shakespeare Association and of its bibliographical wing. The first issue of *SAB* included an article entitled "Why a Shakespeare Association?" by then-President of the SAA Ashley Horace Thorndike, who justified the creation of the SAA and *SAB* as a way to rectify a perceived lack of Shakespeare recognition in the United States, especially compared with other countries:

> In spite of our regard for Shakespeare . . . there are no funds to encourage Shakespearean scholarship or publication of scholarly works. There is no Shakespeare theatre, no playhouse regularly devoting a part of the time to his plays. There is no Shakespeare journal, no adequate Shakespeare *bibliography* . . . . In this and other respects, the United States has lagged far behind England or Germany.[87]

The development of the SAA, then, was a matter of national pride (or, of national anxiety). The desire for an "adequate Shakespeare bibliography" partly spurred the creation of both the SAA, and its "organ," the *SAB*, which included a bibliography from its onset. Shakespeare bibliography is therefore central to our field's professional origins and development. With some irony, the global-facing resource that became the *World Shakespeare Bibliography* emerged from nationalist drive to keep up with Shakespeare studies on the other side of the Atlantic.

Despite its name and stated intention to represent American interests in the world of Shakespeare, the Shakespeare Association of America had a global cast from the very start. SAA's "Articles of Incorporation," printed in the afore-referenced issue 1.1 of the *SAB*, noted that the SAA's objective was "To further the appreciation of Shakespeare as the master-mind which may serve to bring into closer union our English-speaking and other countries – a union built upon a lasting foundation, spiritual and intellectual, which is found in the imaginations, in the minds, and in the hearts of all peoples."[88] In addition to casting its eye across the globe, the SAA attempted to be inclusive in terms of membership (albeit it in a condescending way that did not truly account for "every class"): 1.1's

---

[87] Ashley Horace Thorndike, "Why a Shakespeare Association?" *Shakespeare Association Bulletin* 1, no. 1 (1924): 1–2, 1. Emphasis added.

[88] Shakespeare Association of America, "SAA: Articles of Incorporation," *Shakespeare Association Bulletin* 1, no. 1 (1924): 4–5, 5.

"Report of Membership Committee," noted the paid-up members of the SAA, which "covers every class of Shakespeare lover from the school girl to the scholar."[89] Membership required only that one pay one's dues and have an interest in Shakespeare. The *WSB*'s global scope and inclusive purview, then, can be traced to SAA's interest in uniting people, no matter their country or professional affiliation, through a shared interest in Shakespeare. It must be noted that the SAA's "Articles of Incorporation" are fraught with colonial undertones, suggestive of the way that Shakespeare's supposed "universality" was problematically mapped onto various cultures that saw Shakespeare as a foreign import, rather than as a mirror of their own lives. While the gesture to inclusivity suggests a certain open-mindedness, white Anglo-American scholarship was clearly controlling the discourse and gatekeeping membership in this purportedly "open" association.

In "Recent Work in the Shakespearean Field" (Figure 5), listing the last year's work on Shakespeare and printed in the first issue of the *SAB*, Baugh expresses his aspiration that the bibliography become a regular feature of the journal. The section reprints a portion of Baugh's "American Bibliography" from *PMLA*, demonstrating how different bibliographical organizations dovetail and cooperate with one another. Baugh notes, "A summary of this kind shows how much might be done by the Shakespeare Association to bring the larger circle of Shakespeare lovers full and accurate information concerning the large amount of scholarly production that is appearing."[90] This early bibliography was not yet the orderly resource that the *WSB* would later strive to become: there is no clear organizing principle for Baugh's bibliography, skipping from one topic to the next and back again. It includes non-Shakespearean material, touching on Wyatt, Tottel, Spenser, Sidney, Lyly, Marlowe, and John Heywood, as well as references to broader studies of the Renaissance, such as "Money Lending and Money-Lenders in England during the 16th and 17th centuries," "The Tradition of Angelic Singing in English Drama," and "Theatrical Bill

---

[89] Windsor P. Daggett, "Report of Membership Committee," *Shakespeare Association Bulletin* 1, no. 1 (1924): 15–16, 16.

[90] Albert C. Baugh, "Recent Work in the Shakespearean Field," *Shakespeare Association Bulletin* 1, no. 1 (1924): 17–20, 17.

RECENT WORK IN THE SHAKESPEAREAN FIELD

By Professor ALBERT C. BAUGH

A PART of Professor Albert C. Baugh's "American Bibliography," which appeared in the March issue of the *Publications of the Modern Language Association*, is here reprinted with permission and with thanks. A summary of this kind shows how much might be done by the Shakespeare Association to bring to the larger circle of Shakespeare lovers full and accurate information concerning the large amount of scholarly production that is appearing.

The following abbreviations are used: *PMLA, Publications of the Modern Language Association of America; SP, Studies in Philology; PQ, Philological Quarterly; MLN, Modern Language Notes; JEGP, Journal of English and Germanic Philology; MP, Modern Philology; N&Q, Notes and Queries.*

* * *

T. S. Graves has published his annual bibliography of "Recent Literature of the English Renaissance" (*SP*, XX. 244-92) and Hardin Craig suggests "Some Problems of Scholarship in the Literature of the Renaissance, particularly in the English Field" (*PQ*, I. 81-99). W. L. Bullock finds "The Genesis of the English Sonnet Form" (*PMLA*, XXXVIII. 729-44) in Italian models which Wyatt could have known and which are in the form most commonly adopted by Wyatt. F. M. Padelford studies "The Scansion of Wyatt's Early Sonnets" (*SP*, XX. 137-52) in the light of earlier Tudor verse. H. H. Hudson raises an interesting point in Surrey and Martial" (*MLN*, XXXVIII. 481-3) one of Surrey's translations being found in print ten years before it appeared in Tottel's *Songs and Sonnets*. E. Greenlaw discusses "The Captivity Episode in Sidney's *Arcadia*" (*Manly Ann. Studies*, 54-63). S. L. Wolff contributes a long paper on "The Humanist as Man of Letters: John Lyly" (*Sewanee Rev.*, XXXI. 8-35) and W. P. Mustard comments on Lyly's allusion to "Hippocrates' Twins" (*MLN*, XXXVIII. 313) in *Euphues and his England*. F. I. Carpenter has published a very valuable *Reference Guide to Edmund Spenser* and has written on "Spenser Apocrypha" (*Manly Ann. Studies*, 64-69). M. Y. Hughes tests the supposed relation between "Spenser and the Greek Pastoral Triad" (*SP*, XX. 184-215) and finds a much more immediate indebtedness to the Pleiade. E. Greenlaw writes on "Some Old Religious Cults in Spenser" (*SP*, XX. 216-43) and F. M. Padelford treats of "The Spiritual Allegory of the Faerie Queen, Book One" (*JEGP*, XXII. 1-17). D. T. Starnes in "Purpose in the Writing of History" (*MP*, XX. 281-300) traces the conception of history from Greek times to Sidney as written to furnish examples of virtue to follow and of vice to shun. A. B. Stonex continues his study of "Money Lending and Money-lenders in England during the 16th and 17th Centuries" (*Schelling Ann. Papers*, 263-85) concerning himself in this paper with the non-dramatic literature. E. M. Albright continues her dispute with Pollard "*Ad Imprimendum Solum* Once More" (*MLN*, XXXVIII. 129-40),

Posting in the Age of Elizabeth." For Baugh, the "Shakespearean Field" includes material adjacent to Shakespeare, unlike the *WSB*, which excludes material not explicitly linked to Shakespeare. The Shakespearean content of Baugh's bibliography offers a fascinating snapshot of Shakespeare scholarship in the early twentieth century. It lists Joseph Q. Adams's *Life of William Shakespeare* (deemed to be "a book of the first importance") and two articles about Shakespeare allusions in the seventeenth century (the early twentieth century being the high-water mark of Shakespeare allusion books).[91] Published in 1924, Baugh's bibliography also notes several works published marking the 300th anniversary of the publication of the First Folio the previous year, including an entry on Kaufman's "Celebrating the Tercentenary of a Famous Book." The bibliography also indexes dissertations and includes a substantial section on articles and books on *Hamlet* (on the play's Germanic sources; Hamlet as a "man of action"; the play/character's influence on Romantic thinking; the first quarto of *Hamlet*; *Hamlet* in the Restoration). It does, of course, also list articles and books on other individual Shakespearean plays. After covering Shakespeare, the bibliography returns to non-Shakespearean material, such as scholarship on *The Hog Hath Lost his Pearl*, and Beaumont and Fletcher plays (including Fletcher's contributions to Shakespeare plays). The bibliography also gathers references to scholarship on the performance of Shakespeare plays in Germany, attesting to the scope of Shakespearean bibliography outside of the Anglo-American context. The bibliography's pattern of organization is not obvious or consistent: it does not offer a clear table of contents, index or section headings, and shuttles back and forth between work on Shakespeare and work on non-Shakespearean topics. As we shall see, successive editors of the *World Shakespeare Bibliography* strove to solve this problem by developing a system of organization that was informative and intuitive.

The subsequent few issues of the *Shakespeare Association Bulletin* show the journal experimenting with different ways of approaching and structuring a Shakespeare bibliography. Following 1.1's "Recent Work in the Shakespearean Field," the second issue (1.2, 1925) includes "Our Members in Print," listing articles and books by SAA membership; entries

---

[91] Baugh, "Recent Work in the Shakespearean Field," 18.

are organized by member (not in alphabetical order) – a rather solipsistic way to do Shakespearean bibliography! The third issue of *Shakespeare Association Bulletin* (1.3, 1926) includes the "Classified Index of Shakespeareana in the Periodicals of 1925," by Samuel A. Tannenbaum, listing articles related to Shakespeare published in different journals. For the first time, the bibliography is clearly organized by topic, including headings such as "Authorship Question," "Bibliography" (including other bibliographies, such as Graves, "Recent Literature of the English Renaissance," the German "Shakespeare Bibliographie für 1921–22"), "Biographia and Personalia," "Handwriting," and play and poem titles (*All's Well* to *Venus and Adonis*), with the largest subsection devoted to *Hamlet*. "Staging and Stage History," "Textual Criticism," and a catch-all category under "Miscellaneous" were also featured. *SAB* 1.3 also includes "The Shakespeare Book Shelf," which lists recent book publications and offers brief summaries of each. *Shakespeare Association Bulletin* 2.1 (March 1927) also includes "The Book Shelf," listing titles of recent books along with several paragraphs of explanation for each one, while the *Shakespeare Association Bulletin* 2.2 (June 1927) includes the "Classified Index of Shakespeareana in the Periodicals of 1926," with similar topics as the year previous, and the addition of "Commentary and Criticism," "Knowledge," "Learning," and "Music." Just as the *WSB*'s tags would later shift over time, introducing new subjects as others receded, the early headings here offer a something of a bird's eye view of the priorities of Shakespeare Studies in the early days of the SAA's incorporation.

By 1928, the *SAB* had found a reliable pattern for its bibliography. The Annual Bibliography for 1927 published in *Shakespeare Association Bulletin* in 3.1 (1928) was entitled "A Classified Shakespeare Bibliography for 1927," and compiled by Samuel A. Tannenbaum. Unlike the previous iterations of bibliography in the *Shakespeare Association Bulletin* (which were divided into books and articles in periodicals), this iteration united books and articles, as well as pamphlets and newspapers. The "Classified Shakespeare Bibliography" first lists the abbreviations for journals; the entries are then organized under the following headings: "Allusions," "America," "Art," "Astrology" (with one entry), "Authorship Problems," "Bacon-Shakespeare Controversy," "Bibliography," "Biographia and Personalia," "Botany" (with one entry),

"Burlesques," "Commentary and Criticism," "Criminals and Criminology," "Environment," "Forgeries," "France," "Handwriting," "History," "Humor," "Identity," "Language," "Medical Knowledge," "Plays and Poems" (with each text as a subheading and Falstaff given his own category), "Politics," "Portraits," "Relics," "Religion," "Staging and Stage History," "Stratford-on-Avon," "Study," "Textual Criticism," "Translations," "Translating," "Will," and "Works." The model established in 1928 for Shakespeare bibliography continued for the next two decades.[92]

In the Shakespeare Bibliography for 1935 (published in 1936), Tannenbaum explained the principles of inclusion:

> The following bibliography, based on an examination of the contents of more than 1,300 periodicals and hundreds of books, is a continuation of that published in this Bulletin in January, 1935. Perfunctory notices of books, blurbs, and reviews which contribute nothing new, have not been noted. The names of female writers are distinguished by a colon (instead of a period) after the initial letter of the baptismal name. The titles of books and pamphlets are printed in italics. If no year is mentioned in connection with an item, '1935' is to be understood. Reviews of books are listed (without a preceding number), without title, immediately after the books themselves. The discussion of a book is indicated by printing the title within single quotes.[93]

---

[92] The bibliography's name shifted from "A Classified Shakespeare Bibliography" to "Annual Bibliography of Shakespeariana" to "Shakespeare and His Contemporaries: A Classified Bibliography." See, for instance: "A Classified Shakespeare Bibliography for 1927," *Shakespeare Association Bulletin* 3, no. 1 (1928): 1–21; "Annual Bibliography of Shakespeariana for 1931," *Shakespeare Association Bulletin* 7, no. 1 (1932): 1–46; and "Shakespeare and His Contemporaries: A Classified Bibliography for 1936," *Shakespeare Association Bulletin* 12, no. 1 (1937): 2–34.

[93] Samuel T. Tannenbaum, "Annual Bibliography of Shakespeariana for 1935," *Shakespeare Association Bulletin* 11, no. 1, (1936): 2–32, 2.

Book reviews are included alongside the books they cover. Once again, entries are organized by topic. Shakespeare's contemporaries Beaumont and Fletcher, Chapman, Chettle, and others too many to name, are given their own headings. Of particular note is that women writers are distinguished typographically in the bibliography. Tannenbaum states that, "The names of female writers are distinguished by a colon (instead of a period) after the initial letter of the baptismal name," with no further explanation given for this distinction.[94] While the rationale for distinguishing women scholars typographically is at first unclear, Tannenbaum's emphasis on the "baptismal name" suggests that women were recognized differently because often their names would change over their careers, as when, for instance, they got married.[95] This typographical distinction not only recognizes women's scholarly labor but also marks it as exceptional.

Tannenbaum continued to compile "A Classified Bibliography of Shakespeare and his Contemporaries" until 1944, at which point, he started to share the bibliographical work with his spouse Dorothy Rosenzweig Tannenbaum.[96] She was also responsible for compiling the "Index of Names and Subjects Occurring in the Bibliography of Elizabethan Topics for 1944," and the same Index for the issue published the following year.[97] Rosenzweig Tannenbaum was solely responsible for the Classified Bibliography for 1948.[98] This bibliography includes a note from Tannenbaum: "The Editor expresses his thanks to Mrs. Tannenbaum for compiling the Bibliography for 1948, and is

---

[94] Samuel T. Tannenbaum, "Annual Bibliography of Shakespeariana for 1935," *Shakespeare Association Bulletin* 11, no. 1 (1936), 2.

[95] For more on name changes and bibliography, see Heidi Craig, Laura Estill, and Kris L. May, "A Rationale of Trans-Inclusive Bibliography," *Textual Cultures* 16, no. 2 (2023): 1–28.

[96] We differentiate between Rosenzweig Tannenbaum (Dorothy) and Tannenbaum (Samuel) in our text for clarity, though Dorothy published using only the middle initial "R" rather than "Rosenzweig."

[97] Dorothy R. Tannenbaum, "Index of Names and Subjects: Occurring in the Bibliography of Elizabethan Topics for 1944," *Shakespeare Association Bulletin* 20, no. 1 (1945): 15–21.

[98] Dorothy R. Tannenbaum, "Shakespeare and his Contemporaries (A Classified Bibliography for 1948)," *Shakespeare Association Bulletin* 24, no. 2 (1949): 136–75.

glad to acknowledge aid fully given by Dr. Herman I. Radin, William B. White and Russell N. De Vinney."[99] Tannenbaum acknowledging his wife hearkens to the untold stories of women who assisted their male partners in scholarly labors, sometimes invoked as a nameless "my wife" (if their work was noted at all), as demonstrated in Juliana Dresvina's collection *Thanks for Typing: Remembering Forgotten Women in History*.[100] However, Tannenbam does acknowledge his wife by name; as we can see from the shared citation, Rosenzweig Tannenbaum's active and overt involvement with the bibliography is a notable exception to this otherwise bleak history and can be celebrated as a time when a "helpmate" stepped out of the shadows and into the bibliographical record.

Rosenzweig Tannenbaum's bibliography was the last to appear before *SAB* became *Shakespeare Quarterly* in 1950: fittingly, her bibliography was listed in *Shakespeare Quarterly's* first annual bibliography (published in its second issue). In what follows, we discuss the first quarter century of *SQ*'s annual bibliography, which was indebted to the earlier bibliographies published by the *SAB* in the 1920s, 1930s, and 1940s, and those in turn were inspired by earlier iterations in the twentieth century and before. As we'll cover in the final section of this Element, *SQ*'s annual bibliography would later become the *World Shakespeare Bibliography*.

3.2 The Shakespeare Quarterly *Annual Bibliography, 1950–1976*

The first half of the twentieth century was perhaps the high-water mark of comprehensive enumerative bibliography. Much of this enumerative work was devoted to works of Shakespeare and his dramatic contemporaries. Whereas much of nineteenth-century scholarship had been consumed with matters of aesthetics, well-known textual scholars such as Ronald B. McKerrow, A. W. Pollard, and W. W. Greg, as well as understudied bibliographers such as Henrietta C. Bartlett, devoted their attention to

---

[99] Samuel T. Tannenbaum, in Dorothy R. Tannenbaum, "Shakespeare and his Contemporaries," 136, unnumbered footnote.

[100] Julia Dresvina, *Thanks for Typing: Remembering Forgotten Women in History* (Bloomsbury, 2021).

bibliography both descriptive and enumerative after the turn of the century.[101] The New Bibliographers, including McKerrow, Pollard, and Greg, emphasized inferences that could be made from careful study of the physical book, while Bartlett and Greg dutifully compiled lists of those physical books deemed to be worthy of close study. Bartlett and Pollard's *A Census of Shakespeare's Plays in Quarto 1594–1709* (1916, revised by Bartlett in 1939) lists the locations of known copies of Shakespeare quartos and contains notes on the copies' binding, condition, and completeness.[102] Between 1939 and 1959, W. W. Greg published his authoritative *Bibliography of the English Printed Drama to the Restoration* (1939–1959), a handsomely printed four-volume reference work listing all editions of English drama printed up to 1660, with information about each edition's paratexts, title pages, and public holdings of individual copies. Both Bartlett/Pollard's and Greg's references have been foundational for subsequent scholarship and textual criticism. It is notable that these twentieth-century bibliographies were all compiled in the shadow of the world wars. Scholars have noted how, across time, cultural trauma spurs the compilation of comprehensive bibliographies and other reference works, noting the desire to shore up knowledge in the face of widespread loss.[103] This trend continued into the twentieth century. It is probably not a coincidence that *A World Bibliography of Bibliographies* appeared after the apocalyptic losses of the "Great War" and was then republished after World War II.

Shakespeare Quarterly's first annual bibliography was named "Shakespeare: An Annotated Bibliography for 1949," appearing in *SQ* 1.2, printed in Spring 1950 (Figure 6). It was edited by Sidney Thomas (1915–2009), compiled "in

---

[101] Houghton, "Private Owners, Public Books."

[102] Henrietta C. Bartlett and Alfred Pollard, *A Census of Shakespeare's Plays in Quarto 1594–1709* (Yale University Press, 1916). Revised by Bartlett in 1939.

[103] Trevor Ross discusses the compilation of the first bibliographies in the aftermath of the iconoclasm of the English Reformation in *The Making of the English Literary Canon: From the Middle Ages to the Late Eighteenth Century* (McGill-Queen's Press, 2000), 60–61. Heidi Craig discusses the emergence of the first comprehensive playbook catalogs following the English Civil War in *Theatre Closure*, 27–32.

SHAKESPEARE: AN ANNOTATED BIBLIOGRAPHY FOR 1949

Edited by Sidney Thomas

With the collaboration of: Prof. Sergio Baldi, Univ. of Pisa, Italy; Prof. G. A. Bonnard, Univ. of Lausanne, Switzerland; Prof. Karl Brunner, Univ. of Innsbruck, Austria; Prof. Wolfgang Clemen, Univ. of Münich, Germany; Prof. Juliusz Krzyzanowski, Univ. of Wroclaw, Poland; Prof. P. N. U. Harting, Univ. of Amsterdam, The Netherlands; Prof. Pierre Legouis, Univ. of Lyons, France; Mr. Mogens Müllertz, Copenhagen, Denmark; Mr. Richard Pennington, Univ. Librarian, McGill Univ., Montreal, Canada; Prof. Kristian Smidt, Univ. of Oslo, Norway.

THE following bibliography, which includes only works directly relating to Shakespeare, attempts to list all items of interest to the scholar, the actor and producer, and the general reader. A number of books and articles which may be of use to those concerned with Shakespeare have therefore been included, even though they do not represent original contributions to knowledge or criticism. Such items, however, as journalistic reviews of productions or books, or brief popular articles, have generally been omitted. New printings of previously issued editions or studies are not listed unless there has been substantial revision or expansion. All reviews have been grouped under the books they deal with, even if these books have been included in previous bibliographies. In such instances, however, the description of the book has been given in short form. The year 1949 is always to be understood, if no other year is specifically mentioned.

The annotations are designed to indicate the subject-matter or argument of the items listed. In no sense are they intended as criticisms of the books or articles which they explain. Certain significant articles are not annotated because their titles sufficiently indicate their content. The length of the annotation is also no guide to the importance of the item. Several books are listed without annotation because they have not yet become available here.

The editor wishes to thank the members of the staffs of the Queens College Library, the Columbia University Library, and the New York Public Library for their many courtesies. Dr. Herman T. Radin of New York City has generously submitted his own independent listing of many items. The distinguished scholars from many countries who have cooperated in the preparation of this bibliography have contributed greatly towards broadening its scope and increasing its usefulness.

The editor would appreciate receiving copies of books, and off-prints of articles and reviews dealing with Shakespeare, in order to ensure as complete a coverage of the field as possible.

cooperation" with academics across Europe (Italy, Austria, West Germany, Poland, the Netherlands, France, Denmark, Norway) as well as from Canada and the United States, the latter with contributing staff members from academic libraries. The specter of global politics stalked the "Annotated Bibliography" from the very start: while the bulk of academics and librarians were operating in Western Europe, Prof. Juliusz Krzyzanowski, of the University of Wroclaw, Poland, was behind the Iron Curtain. The Cold War irreparably shaped Thomas's life, too. Thomas was a renowned Shakespeare scholar who was ousted from the profession due to his political ideals. His obituary notes that Thomas stood "up to the scourge of McCarthyism in the 1950s [and] he sacrificed his academic job rather than agree to 'name names.'"[104] It seems inevitable that global politics would shape a bibliography whose mandate was global inclusivity and which would come to include Shakespeare scholarship from every continent; from every country in North America, South America, and Europe and nearly every country in Asia, Africa, and Australasia; and written in over 120 languages.[105]

From the start, comprehensiveness through collaboration was the annual bibliography's stated ideal and workflow. The first bibliography of 1950 acknowledges its acquisition of copies of books and off-prints of articles and reviews "in order to ensure as complete a coverage of the field as possible."[106] The first bibliography also acknowledged the purpose of collaboration as "broadening [the bibliography's] scope and increasing its usefulness."[107] The scope was to capture all works "directly relating to Shakespeare," with an "attempt to list all items of interest to the scholar, the

---

[104] "Sidney Thomas Obituary," *Syracuse Post Standard* (November 8, 2009), obits.syracuse.com/us/obituaries/syracuse/name/sidney-thomas-obituary?id=17083058.

[105] Laura Estill, "Digital Bibliography and Global Shakespeare," *Scholarly and Research Communication* 5, no. 4 (2014), src-online.ca/index.php/src/article/view/187/358.

[106] Sidney Thomas, "Shakespeare: An Annotated Bibliography for 1949," *Shakespeare Quarterly* 1, no. 2 (1950): 97–120, 97.

[107] Thomas, "Shakespeare: An Annotated Bibliography for 1949," 97.

actor and producer, and the general reader."[108] Features distinctive to the present-day *WSB* are recognizable in this earliest of iterations, including the comprehensive listing of book reviews for titles related to Shakespeare. In the annual bibliography, reviews of a given book were listed under the titles they discuss (even if the book itself was covered in an earlier iteration of the bibliography). As was later practice, annotations were written to be informative, not critical. "In no sense," Thomas explained, "are they intended as criticisms of the books or articles which they explain."[109] Even as the bibliography duly indexed work on discredited theories (such as Oxfordian theories of Shakespearean publication), it did so without judgment, allowing readers to draw their own conclusions.

Most of the features of the first annual bibliography endured into its second installment, "Shakespeare: An Annotated Bibliography for 1950," published in 1951.[110] This issue echoes the rationale of the first in its "attempt to list all items of interest to the scholar, the actor and producer, and the general reader."[111] It also articulates the bibliography's need for a scope that is paradoxically both broad and narrow: the preliminary matter reports its limited inclusion of previously issued editions or studies to substantially revised or expanded ones with exception of "reissues of editions and translations" published in countries or languages different from the original publication. Moreover, the bibliography notes its intention to include works on the same topic, "even though they do not represent original contributions to knowledge or criticism," while also omitting "journalistic reviews of productions or books, or brief popular articles."[112]

The second iteration of the bibliography also saw the expansion of international contributors beyond Europe and North America, with contributions from South Africa and Turkey. The third iteration, published in 1952, featured for the first time contributors from Japan and India, and the

[108] Thomas, "Shakespeare: An Annotated Bibliography for 1949," 97.
[109] Thomas, "Shakespeare: An Annotated Bibliography for 1949," 97.
[110] Thomas, "Shakespeare: An Annotated Bibliography for 1950," *Shakespeare Quarterly* 2, no. 2 (1951): 143–70.
[111] Thomas, "Shakespeare: An Annotated Bibliography for 1950," 143.
[112] Thomas, "Shakespeare: An Annotated Bibliography for 1950," 143.

bibliography from 1953 added a contributor from Yugoslavia.[113] At the time of writing, the bibliography's international contributors, past and present, represent fifty-seven nations and regions.

In 1955, for the Annual Bibliography's sixth iteration, Thomas was replaced as editor by Paul Jorgensen (1916–2000), a Californian who was educated and who worked in California's UC system. The bibliography for that year acknowledged the "continual support of the University of California Library and the Huntington Library."[114] Under Jorgensen's editorship, the Annual Bibliography retained much of its prefatory matter explaining its rationale, audience, and scope. On the inclusion of performance reviews, Jorgensen explained that, "although no attempt has been made to achieve exhaustive coverage of journalistic reviews of productions or books, there will usually be found a representative body of such selections – particularly those of foreign origin and those dealing with Shakespearian festivals."[115] In 1959, we see for the first time the addition of an associate editor, Robert Dent, who became editor in 1960, and was joined in 1965 by Rudolph F. Habenicht of Simon Fraser University (British Columbia, Canada) as associate editor, who in turn became editor in 1966. (Habenicht's editorship was "Dented" by that previous editor's return for one year in 1970.)

It was under Habenicht's editorship that the Annotated Bibliography, already global in scope, announced this in its title. In 1966, "Shakespeare: An Annotated Bibliography" was renamed "Shakespeare: An Annotated World Bibliography."[116] When Dent briefly returned as editor in 1970, the bibliography temporarily reverted to "Shakespeare: An Annotated

---

[113] Thomas, "Shakespeare: An Annotated Bibliography for 1951," *Shakespeare Quarterly* 3, no. 2 (1952): 149–84; and "Shakespeare: An Annotated Bibliography for 1952," *Shakespeare Quarterly* 4, no. 2 (1953): 219–54.

[114] Paul Jorgensen, "Shakespeare: An Annotated Bibliography for 1954," *Shakespeare Quarterly* 6, no. 2 (1955): 201–45.

[115] Jorgensen, "Shakespeare: An Annotated Bibliography for 1955," *Shakespeare Quarterly* 7, no. 2 (1956): 291–349, 291.

[116] Rudolph E. Habenicht, "Shakespeare: An Annotated World Bibliography for 1965," *Shakespeare Quarterly*, 17, no. 3 (1966): 213–341.

Bibliography."[117] In the bibliography published in 1969, the "Annotated World Bibliography" offers special thanks to Professor Harrison T. Meserole for "galley proofs of useful sections of the 1967 and 1968 *PLMA* International Bibliographies."[118] Meserole would later become the Bibliography's editor, and would usher it into the digital age. This special thanks is the first time Merserole's contribution was noted in print. Similar thanks were offered in the 1970 iteration, when Bruce Nesbitt became assistant editor. By 1972, Nesbitt was editor, with Rudolph E. Habenicht serving as chairman of the committee for correspondents, the new position suggestive of how much bibliography had expanded globally.[119]

The 1972 "Annotated World Bibliography" announced its and *SQ*'s association with the Folger Shakespeare Library, declaring the "humanistic importance of enumerative bibliography: as a gentle art, and as a rigorous discipline."[120] Noting that the bibliography had started to use computational processes for its compilation, it continues, "Professor Harrison Meserole's advice has been especially welcome, on both the horrors and the benefits of using modern data-processing systems."[121] In this issue, Nesbitt candidly describes the challenges of compiling the bibliography, related to labor and expense:

> I am responsible for gathering two-thirds of the entries below and for annotating most items published in areas not covered by the Committee of Correspondents, including the United Kingdom and the United States. After three years with the

---

[117] Robert Dent, "Shakespeare: An Annotated Bibliography," *Shakespeare Quarterly* 21, no. 3 (1970): 280–7.

[118] Habenicht, "Shakespeare: An Annotated World Bibliography for 1968," *Shakespeare Quarterly* 20, no. 3 (1969): 265–374, 267.

[119] Habenicht, "Shakespeare: An Annotated World Bibliography for 1969," *Shakespeare Quarterly* 21, no. 3 (1970), 255–381; Habenicht, "Shakespeare: An Annotated World Bibliography for 1971," *Shakespeare Quarterly* 23, no. 3 (1972): 273–382.

[120] Bruce Nesbitt, "Shakespeare: An Annotated World Bibliography for 1971," *Shakespeare Quarterly* 23, no. 3 (1972): 273–382, 275.

[121] Nesbitt, "Shakespeare: An Annotated World Bibliography for 1971," 275.

Bibliography, also voluntarily undertaken, I remain convinced that this work must be shared more equitably .... I am most concerned about problems of indexing, particularly if financing can be obtained for the preparation of a cumulative *Shakespeare Quarterly* Bibliography.[122]

In the next issue, Nesbitt elaborates further, calling for "the cooperation of scholars" in improving "the scope and accuracy of the Bibliography": "All Shakespearians interested in contributing information on specific journals or books are encouraged to write me."[123] In the subsequent issue, Nesbitt offered a vivid description of the bibliographer's task:

All enumerative bibliographies are genial dragons, devouring time, haunting dreams, breathing fire on other plans. That the pursuit of the dragon is addictive, on the other hand, can be demonstrated by my founding an annual annotated bibliography of Canadian literature/litterature canadienne, modeled on the style of this Bibliography. And that my other dragon is already nearly the size of this one is surely evidence of the hazards to the peculiar quest of all bibliographers.[124]

Nesbitt also outlined the accomplishment of the past years' goals "to enhance the accuracy of the Bibliography, and of its indexes; to develop a program which will allow the future mechanization of some aspects of compiling the Bibliography; and to ensure the orderly transfer of the Bibliography from the Shakespeare Association of America to the Folger Shakespeare Library."[125] In 1975, Habenicht returned as editor with

---

[122] Nesbitt, "Shakespeare: An Annotated World Bibliography for 1971," 275.

[123] Nesbitt, "Shakespeare: An Annotated World Bibliography for 1972," *Shakespeare Quarterly* 24, no. 4 (1973), 487–600, 489.

[124] Rudolph E. Habenicht, "Shakespeare: An Annotated World Bibliography for 1973," *Shakespeare Quarterly* 25, no. 4 (1974): 439–545, 441.

[125] Habenicht, "Shakespeare: An Annotated World Bibliography for 1973," 441.

Thomas F. Grieve.[126] This iteration was the first to thank the "assistance of an International Committee of Correspondents" and also notes that the "total number of entries, which include some few entered a day after final numbering, represents the largest *Shakespeare Quarterly* Bibliography since the 1964 Quatercentenary behemoth."[127]

In 1976, John F. Andrews, editor of *Shakespeare Quarterly*, in "From the Editor: The 'New' World Shakespeare Bibliography," announced the appointment of Meserole as editor, joined by Priscilla J. Letterman, and acknowledged Penn State University for its support in the compilation of the bibliography.[128] It also anticipated the bibliography's latter-day name (*World Shakespeare Bibliography*), which endures to the present, but which was not officially used until 1979.[129] This editor's note describes the Bibliography as a "valuable tool for advanced research" and notes Meserole's ambition for the next issue: "to employ full computerization, thereby augmenting the efficiency and flexibility with which entries may be recorded and retrieved for scholarly purposes."[130] With this in mind, the Bibliography adopted the *MLA Style Sheet*'s entry format to facilitate future computerization of data; the attending Bibliography notes Meserole's credentials as "Editor of the massive MLA Bibliography" for over a decade.[131] The Bibliography for 1975 was reorganized into two divisions: (1) General Shakespeareana (including ten categories related to publication, productions of Shakespeare's plays, and reviews of productions); and (2) Studies of

[126] Thomas F. Grieve and Rudolph E. Habenicht, "Shakespeare: An Annotated World Bibliography for 1974," *Shakespeare Quarterly* 26, no. 4 (1975): 325–461.

[127] Grieve and Habenicht, "Shakespeare: An Annotated World Bibliography for 1974," 326.

[128] John F. Andrews, "From the Editor: The 'New' World Shakespeare Bibliography," *Shakespeare Quarterly* 27, no. 4 (1976): 387.

[129] Harrison T. Meserole and John B. Smith, "Shakespeare: Annotated World Bibliography for 1978," *Shakespeare Quarterly* 30, no. 4 (1979): 454–69; where it is explained that John B. Smith, "serves as Technical Editor for the World Shakespeare Bibliography."

[130] Andrews, "From the Editor: The 'New' World Shakespeare Bibliography," 387.

[131] Harrison T. Meserole, "Shakespeare: Annotated World Bibliography for 1975," *Shakespeare Quarterly* 27, no. 4 (1976): 389–96, 389.

Particular Works (listed under titles of individual plays and poems, as well as dramatic genres). The Bibliography omits overlapping items, explaining that "each essay or book [is] listed only once, in the category where we believe it will be sought for by the largest group of users of the Bibliography," but some entries fitting other categories would be cross-referenced, thus modeling another notable feature of the present-day online *WSB*.[132]

Even with his immense ambition and talent for bibliography, Meserole introduced the Bibliography with typical humility: "It would be comforting to believe, as does Proteus (*TGV*) that 'were man but constant, he were perfect.' Bibliographers, though they strive for perfection, know better. The editor of this Bibliography will be grateful, therefore, to colleagues who discover errors and report corrections."[133] In a retrospective issue reflecting on the history of *Shakespeare Quarterly* and its predecessor, the *Shakespeare Association Bulletin*, *SQ* editor Andrews noted that "tradition – a handing down of cultural values from one generation to another – is an appropriate term to apply to the continuity one observes when leafing through back issues of the *Bulletin* and *Quarterly*. Much of what characterizes the current journal was present – or at least latent – in the beginning."[134] Central to this consistency was *SQ*'s Bibliography. Andrews's potted history is thus worth quoting:

> The annual bibliography of Shakespeare studies, commenced in 1926 under the direction of Dr. Samuel A. Tannenbaum, has continued for more than five decades [and] has grown enormously ... filling entire issues of the periodical as early as 1928 ... [The] Bibliography grew by leaps and bounds with a succession of Bibliographers (Robert W. Dent, Rudolph E. Habenicht, Bruce Nesbitt) each widening the net and adding his own refinements to an instrument of scholarship that was increasingly depended upon the world over ... [A]n ever-expanding, ever more

---

[132] Meserole, "Shakespeare: Annotated World Bibliography for 1975," 389.
[133] Meserole, "Shakespeare: Annotated World Bibliography for 1975," 390.
[134] John F. Andrews, "From the Editor: Thirty Years – And More," *Shakespeare Quarterly* 30, no. 4 (1979): 451–3.

sophisticated *World Shakespeare Bibliography* under the direction of Harry Meserole.[135]

While Andrews was looking back, Meserole and his team were looking resolutely forward. With Meserole at the helm and an ambition for full computerization, the *WSB* was on the cusp of its next significant leap forward. As both this prehistory and history of the *WSB* suggest, Shakespearean bibliography relied on collaboration and human labor, which sometimes went unacknowledged, as we can see, for instance, from Rosenzweig Tannenbaum's omission from Andrews's retrospective. And yet, despite the sometimes thankless and always daunting nature of Shakespeare bibliography, this "genial dragon" was sure to give its keepers ample diversion and occupation.

4 Regional Shakespeare Bibliographies: Case Studies in Scope and Scholarly Attention

Previous sections of this Element have focused on Shakespeare bibliography in British, American, and German contexts and how they aimed to capture all Shakespeare publications. The resulting ambit, then, is always global: we can see how these models led to the *World Shakespeare Bibliography*, which will be discussed at length in the next section.

At this Element's center, we turn to regional bibliographies. Such bibliographies emerged to catalog performances and scholarship based outside of the Anglophone world. Even with the *World Shakespeare Bibliography* (emphasis added), today, these bibliographies are still pivotal to scholarship because their scope can extend to material not covered by the *WSB* but which captures approaches to Shakespeare in local and regional contexts: for instance, MA theses, newspaper articles, and most university productions. Indeed, some of the *WSB*'s international correspondents are the same scholars who maintain regional bibliographies.

The regional and thematic Shakespeare bibliographies discussed in this section stand in the middle of our book on purpose: while sometimes these smaller lists are compiled away from the main centers of scholarship, they

---

[135] Andrews, "From the Editor: Thirty Years – And More," 451–3.

are central to Shakespearean bibliography because they show that how we choose to make our lists matters for the claims we make – about the value of Shakespeare or the importance of turning to scholarship from a particular region. Likewise, the examples in this section offer a midpoint to our book as they start to move from printed bibliographies to digital. We see how changing technological affordances change users' expectations, as well as how those compiling bibliographies are able to collaborate.

What follows is not an exhaustive list or consideration of all regional Shakespeare bibliographies, but rather, case studies that emphasize the key themes of this volume: these bibliographies are created by people; creating a bibliography argues for the items listed as worthy of scholarly consideration; and there is no one-size-fits-all technology appropriate for cataloging work in Shakespeare studies. As of 2025, there were over 680 items tagged as "bibliographies and checklists" listed in the *WSB*, such as Hansjürgen Blinn's *The German Shakespeare*, Mahmoud F. Al-Shetawi's "Shakespeare's Journey into the Arab World: An Initial Bibliography," and Krystyna Kujawińska Courtney's *Polska bibliografia szekspirowska [Polish Shakespeare Bibliography] 1980–2000* – not to mention the regional bibliographies that predate the *WSB*'s 1960 start date, such as Percy J. Marks's *Australasian Shakespeareana* (1915).[136]

As the hundreds of bibliographies listed in the *World Shakespeare Bibliography* attest, the case studies here are not comprehensive. These were selected because they showcase different ways that bibliographies position Shakespeare globally: Japanese Shakespeare bibliography, for instance, highlights Shakespeare's importance in a non-Western culture,

---

[136] Hansjürgen Blinn, *Der deutsche Shakespeare – The German Shakespeare* (E. Schmidt, 1993); Mahmoud F. Al-Shetawi, "Shakespeare's Journey into the Arab World: An Initial Bibliography," *Shakespeare Yearbook* 13 (2002): 442–99; Krystyna Kujawińska Courtney, *Polska bibliografia szekspirowska 1980–2000 [Polish Shakespeare Bibliography* 1980–2000] (Zaklad Narodowy imienia Ossolinskich, 2007); Percy J. Marks, *Australasian Shakespeareana: A Bibliography of Books, Pamphlets, Magazine Articles, &c., That Have Been Printed in Australia, and New Zealand, Dealing with Shakespeare and His Works* (Tyrrell's, 1915).

while also underlining how regional translations, adaptations, performances, and scholarship contribute to Shakespeare studies more broadly. Turning to Shakespeare bibliography in South Africa offers an exemplar of thriving Shakespeare studies in the global South, while also acknowledging Shakespeare's thorny position as a canonical writer in English-colonized countries. The examples of Shakespeare bibliography in Spain and Catalonia point to flourishing European bibliographic traditions beyond the Anglo and German conventions explored at length earlier in this Element and remind us that regional bibliography is not necessarily defined by national borders. This section concludes by pointing to the role of technological change in broadening the scope of Shakespearean bibliography, particularly regional Shakespearean bibliographies.

While many Shakespeare bibliographies that approach Shakespearean scholarship from a regional, cultural, and linguistic perspective are omitted due to space constraints, the ones we cover here demonstrate how regional bibliographies curate a vision of and argue for the importance of geographically situated contributions to Shakespeare studies beyond the traditional strongholds of the field. As Global Shakespeare studies continues to grow as a field of inquiry, so too will the bibliographies, databases, and lists that support it. These case studies invite further scholarship on regional Shakespeare bibliographies, which will need to be attuned to regional and cultural particularities, but might also trace similarities in different traditions and contribute to the growing field of Global Shakespeare studies.

4.1 Japan

Kaori Ashizu points out that, in the 1930s, bibliographies showed the importance of Shakespeare to Japan and Japan to Shakespeare. Ashizu points to Takemi Yamaguchi and Sanki Ichikawa's *Nihon Sheikusupia Shoshi* [*A Japanese Shakespeare-Bibliography*] (published in *Eigo Kenkyu* [*The Study of English*], 1931–33) and Yamaguchi's *Nihon Shaou Shomoku Shuran* [*A Catalog of Books relating to Shakespeare in Japan*] (1933) as part of the movement to emphasize Japanese Shakespeare scholarship and productions."[137] In 1940, Minoru Toyoda published his monograph, *Shakespeare in Japan: An Historical Survey*, which included a "Japanese Shakespeare Bibliography" at the end of the volume. This paratext itself concluded by listing three bibliographies, the two mentioned by Ashizu above and "A Shakespeare-Bibliography" (1906) by Bin Ueda, a noted translator and scholar.[138] This overview does not mention all of the scholarship about Shakespeare in Japan, nor even all the bibliographies; rather, it points to some bibliographies that trace Japanese scholarship about Shakespeare and Shakespeare performance in Japan.

The tradition of creating bibliographies about Shakespeare and Japan continues to this day. The *World Shakespeare Bibliography*, for instance, relies on Takashi Sasaki's periodical bibliography published in *Shakespeare News From Japan*, which began in 1991(covering works published through 1989).[139] The volume of material about Shakespeare produced in Japan is vast. Sasaki also produced multiple standalone bibliographies, such as *Nihon sheikusupia sōran* [*A Survey of Shakespeare in Japan*] (1990, with a second part appearing in 1994), which gathered and expanded the materials he collected in his periodical bibliographies.[140] His *Nihon Sheikusupia kenkyū shoshi (Heisei-hen)* [*Japanese Shakespeare Research Bibliography (Heisei Edition)*] required 500 pages to cover just 20 years: 1989–2009.[141] To date, the *WSB* has indexed materials in 22 volumes of *Shakespeare News from Japan*, covering 1989–2012.

---

[137] Kaori Ashizu, "What's *Hamlet* to Japan?" *HamletWorks* 2014, https://server-66-113-234-189.da.direct/global-language.com/html/ENFOLDED/BIBL/____HamJap.htm (translations in the original).

[138] Toyoda Minoru, *Shakespeare in Japan: An Historical Survey*, reprinted from *Transactions of the Japan Society of London* 26 [1940].

[139] *Shakespeare News from Japan*, vol. 1, introduction by Kosai Ishihara (Komazawa University Shakespeare Institute, 1991).

[140] Takashi Sasaki, *Nihon sheikusupia sōran* [*A Survey of Shakespeare in Japan*] (Elpis, 1990); *Nihon sheikusupia sōran 2* [*A Survey of Shakespeare in Japan 2*] (Elpis, 1995). The expanded CD-ROM version of these works (Elpis, 2005) covered from 1840–2003; for more on CD-ROMs and Shakespearean bibliography, see the next section of this Element.

[141] Takashi Sasaki, *Nihon Sheikusupia kenkyū shoshi (Heisei-hen)[A Bibliography of Shakespeare Studies in Japan (Heisei Period)]* (Econ, 2009).

Sasaki's bibliographies are not entirely absorbed by or replaced by the *WSB*, however, since Sasaki's bibliographies include materials not covered in the *WSB*, such as undergraduate theses. The *WSB*'s coverage of works from Japan is made possible by Sasaki's painstaking labor. As with so many of the Shakespeareans who have contributed to the *WSB*, simply listing Sasaki as an international correspondent seems inadequate when measured against the substance of their contributions to making regional scholarship findable to a broader audience.

Shoichiro Kawai, writing about Shakespeare productions in 2014 and 2015, notes that "there are countless Shakespeare productions at Tokyo and it seems they are increasing in number."[142] Turning to existing bibliographies and their contents over the years is one way to count those productions that Kawai, quoting Feste, sees "shin[ing] every where."[143] Sasaki's bibliography, for instance, has been used as the basis of quantitative and qualitative analysis, as in Kosai Ishihara and Osamu Hirokawa's "A Survey of Shakespeare Performance in Japan 2001–2010."[144] What is included in bibliographies is what gets counted when we do our research: it is what these reference works make visible that we then make accounts of in our scholarship. Until Smith's mid twentieth-century *Classified Shakespeare Bibliography*, Japanese Shakespeare, like most Asian Shakespeare scholarship, was almost altogether overlooked in existing bibliographies, even ones that purported to have global scopes. This is why it is crucial for bibliographers to track scholarship in their own language(s) and regions and why, as we will discuss, the international correspondent model is still in use at the *World Shakespeare Bibliography*.

Ashizu's formulation continues to hold true: bibliographies show the importance of Shakespeare in Japan and also of the contributions from Japan that, in turn, support global scholarship. The bibliography of Shakespeare studies in Japan, that is, finding and listing Japanese

---

[142] Shoichiro Kawai, "Some Japanese Shakespeare Productions in 2014–15, " *Multicultural Shakespeare* 14 (2016): 13–28, 27.

[143] Kawai, "Some Japanese Shakespeare Productions," 27.

[144] Kosai Ishihara and Osamu Hirokawa, "A Survey of Shakespearean Performances in Japan from 2001–2010," *Komazawa University Foreign Language Studies* 16 (2014): 1–44.

contributions to global Shakespeare, outlines a history of Shakespeare studies in Japan while also inviting scholars to write additional histories. While Japan's history of Shakespearean engagement will be, of course, unique and situated, it shows how tracing a Shakespearean scholarship with national and linguistic boundaries is important.

4.2 South Africa

Like Japanese bibliographies to Japan, South African Shakespeare bibliographies showcase the importance of South African contributions to the global study of Shakespeare. For instance, in 1988, the reference staff at the Durban Municipal Library collaborated with their counterparts at other South African libraries to create "A Bibliography of Translations of Shakespeare's Plays into Southern African Languages."[145] This list was organized by translator, but users can easily scan the list to find languages of translation (including Afrikaans, Southern Sotho, and Zulu). This bibliography also clearly lists which libraries held copies of these translations, making it relatively straightforward for users to find a nearby copy. As we saw earlier with *Shakespeare Jahrbuch*, catalogs and bibliographies coexist and overlap. This detailed list included some short biographies and images of translators. By making this list in English and publishing it in *Shakespeare in Southern Africa*, a respected academic journal, the bibliography was designed to reach scholars and other librarians. In short, this bibliography celebrated translators while also facilitating access to their works.

Bibliography was an important part of *Shakespeare in Southern Africa* from the outset. In the first issue (1987), the Department of Librarianship at Rhodes University in South Africa prepared "A Shakespeare Bibliography of Periodical Publications in South Africa in 1985 and 1986."[146] Like the bibliography of South African translations, the labor behind this reference work was credited to

---

[145] Reference Staff of the Durban Municipal Library, "A Bibliography of Translations of Shakespeare's Plays into Southern African Languages," *Shakespeare in Southern Africa* 2 (1988): 124–30.

[146] Department of Librarianship, Rhodes University, "A Shakespeare Bibliography of Periodical Publications in South Africa in 1985 and 1986," *Shakespeare in Southern Africa* 1 (1987): 85–7.hdl.handle.net/10520/AJA1011582X_117.

a collective, emphasizing the collaborative nature of compiling. This three-page list included a short annotation about most publications, a practice rapidly dropped. Although the rationale for which publications were included is not clearly stated anywhere, the list highlighted publications by scholars based at South African universities, as well as publications that have appeared in South African journals such as *UNISA English Studies* and reviews and articles in major South African newspapers such as the *Mail & Guardian* (Johannesburg). Over the years, the annual bibliography was primarily compiled by Cecilia Blight (sometimes credited as Celia). The final version of this bibliography appeared in 2009, prepared by Timothy Hacksley.[147]

After its first issue, the South African Shakespeare bibliography self-indexed pieces published in *Shakespeare in Southern Africa*. This showcased not just a region's scholars, or scholarship in a particular language, or publications about a specific topic. It also celebrated the publications that were published in a particular region – which, as we all know, appear thanks to the labor and contributions from multiple people at various stages of publication, from editorial management to copyediting and typesetting. In Blight's 1995 bibliography, for instance, we see listed pieces by both Stephen Greenblatt and Werner Habicht that appeared in Volume 8 of *Shakespeare in Southern Africa*.[148] Neither article ("Remnants of the Sacred in Early Modern England" and "Shakespeare in Divided Germany," respectively) is about South Africa or regional readings; neither scholar was South African or based at a South African university. Blight's bibliography argued that these works are important because of *where* they were published: South Africa. The bibliography valued the scholarship its journal published because of where it was published and who did the non-authorial publication work.

The South African Shakespeare bibliography also included materials outside the scope of the *World Shakespeare Bibliography*. The 2001 bibliography, prepared by Blight, listed a number of Afrikaans works, such as the tantalizingly titled, "Sexy Candice se Geheime Liefde: Sy's Blond en Pragtig

[147] Timothy Hacksley, "A Bibliography of South African Shakespeare Publications in 2008," *Shakespeare in Southern Africa* 21 (2009): 101–3.

[148] Celia Blight, "A Shakespeare Bibliography of Periodical Publications in South Africa in 1995," *Shakespeare in Southern Africa* 9 (1996): 97–8.

en Sy Gaan Sorg dat Shakespeare Nooit Weer Dieselfde sal Wees Nie [Sexy Candice's Secret Love: She's blonde and beautiful and she's going to make sure Shakespeare will never be the same again.]."[149] This piece, possibly a production review or teaser, appeared in *Huisgenoot*, a weekly magazine aimed at the general public, with "the highest circulation figures of any South African magazine."[150] Most popular magazine articles are excluded from the *WSB*. (This is your call, dear reader, to create a bibliography of Shakespeare articles in teen magazines from the 1990s!) Today, in 2026, despite the popularity of *Huisgenoot*, the digitized back-catalog does not yet go back to 2001, and the only Google search result for this title is Blight's bibliography. The inaccessibility of this article demonstrates that the use of bibliographies sometimes requires digitization to support scholarship otherwise enabled by these reference works. The inverse is also true: with increasing digitization, we will need ongoing bibliographical work to help us navigate the expanding sea of content.

Shakespearean bibliography is political: for instance, the bibliographies of Shakespeare in South Africa began to appear at the end of Apartheid and continued to be published for decades. Language politics in South Africa is fraught and was particularly challenging during Apartheid; for bibliographers to list translations, criticism, and performances in languages beyond English was to legitimize their contributions and bring them to the attention of a broader audience. Furthermore, Zulu Shakespeare in South Africa is a form of political and cultural resistance, and tracing its history gives voice to that resistance and broadens its impact by making it findable and knowable beyond its original contexts. Online projects that recuperate or digitize regional Shakespeare materials, including scholarship and performance, can likewise contribute to presenting them to global audiences, yet these projects can too often be siloed. As the case of the South African Shakespeare bibliography underscores, each bibliography is created by decisions about scope that affects

---

[149] Cecilia Blight, "A Shakespeare Bibliography of Periodical Publications in South Africa in 2001," *Shakespeare in Southern Africa* 14 (2002): 77–8.

[150] "Huisgenoot," *Wikipedia*, accessed December 2024, wikipedia.org/wiki/Huisgenoot.

what gets included or excluded: in this case, it is *where* a work is published that is valued. The work of bibliography is to make materials discoverable, which is inherently political.

4.3 Spain and Catalonia

Ángel-Luis Pujante and Juan F. Cerdá's monumental *Shakespeare en España: Bibliografía Anotada Bilingue | Shakespeare in Spain: An Annotated Bilingual Bibliography* also demonstrates how our bibliographies shape scholarly narratives.[151] In English and Spanish, presented on facing pages, this bibliography includes 600 chronologically organized and annotated entries, as well as 1,000 unannotated entries listed at the end. The editors thus shaped the volume's emphasis by choosing which pieces were worth annotating. The editors explained that they annotate scholarly works but not articles about Shakespeare in the popular press; they also chose to emphasize scholarship that takes a literary approach (and not, for instance, a linguistic approach using Shakespeare's plays to better understand early modern English). These editorial decisions, including what to annotate and how to organize the volume, influence how users perceive the value of the items listed – and provide some insight about regional priorities.

Pujante and Cerdá organized their bibliography chronologically, which spotlights early Spanish scholars writing about Shakespeare, starting with Francisco Mariano Nifo's [*The Spanish nation defended* . . .] in 1764. This start date also emphasizes how this bibliography builds directly on earlier scholarship, such as Pujante and Laura Campillo's *Shakespeare en España: Textos 1764-1916*, which opens with a selection of Nifo's text and, by extension, defines the beginnings of Shakespeare scholarship in the region.[152] Francesca Rayner points out that by ordering the volume chronologically, Pujante and Cerdá "might seem to construct a narrative of inevitable progress towards the quantitative and qualitative consecration of Spanish studies in Shakespeare in

---

[151] Ángel-Luis Pujante and Juan F. Cerdá, eds., *Shakespeare en España: Bibliografía Anotada Bilingue | Shakespeare in Spain: An Annotated Bilingual Bibliography* (Universidad de Murcia and Universidad de Granada, 2015).

[152] Ángel-Luis Pujante and Laura Campillo, *Shakespeare en España: Textos 1764–1916* (Universidad de Murcia and Universidad de Granada, 2007).

the 1990s, which also coincides with the greater consolidation of Shakespeare studies in Spanish universities." She notes that editors include more entries from the 1980s and 1990s than from any other periods.[153] Rayner notes that the editors acknowledge the boom in Shakespeare scholarship at this time. After all, it is only because Pujante and Cerdá listed these publications in the first place that they can draw the quantitative conclusion that "there were as many publications on Shakespeare during the 1990s in Spain as in the first six decades of the twentieth century."[154] A comprehensive bibliography thus allows us to make quantitative claims about trends and emphases in scholarship and can show if our use and citation of that scholarship (in, say, anthologies or editions) is truly representative.

Pujante and Cerdá used their bibliography to show which of Shakespeare's works Spanish scholars (i.e., "written in Spain or by Spaniards") focused on over time, showing that "Shakespeare begins and ends these three centuries as an author of tragedies."[155] They pointed out that *Hamlet*, *Romeo and Juliet*, *Othello*, and *Macbeth* were mainstays through the nineteenth and early twentieth centuries, while the late twentieth-century boom in scholarship brought a renewed interest in other plays, such as *Coriolanus* and *Richard II*.[156] Pujante and Cerdá suggested the need for additional regional bibliographies, "not so much to measure ourselves against others as to develop a spirit of cooperation which, some day, will enable us to write the history of Shakespeare on the European continent, and, by extension, in the rest of the world."[157] Yes, we need more national/regional Shakespeare bibliographies – though bless the soul who will have to disambiguate the entries and who might wonder why, for instance, some of Jan Kott's work is included in the Shakespeare in Spain bibliography (because, as Jesús Tronch points out, it was published in Valencia), as well as in the Polish

---

[153] Francesca Rayner, review of *Shakespeare En Espãna: Bibliografia Anotada Bilingue | Shakespeare in Spain: An Annotated Bilingual Bibliography*, ed. Ángel-Luis Pujante and Juan F. Cerdá, *Cahiers Élisabéthains* 89, no. 1 (2016): 136–8, 137.

[154] Rayner, review, 137.

[155] Pujante and Cerdá, *Shakespeare en España*, X and XL.

[156] Pujante and Cerdá, *Shakespeare en España*, XL.

[157] Pujante and Cerdá, *Shakespeare en España*, XLII.

bibliography and also in the bibliographies in all the other languages his work might have been translated into.[158] Regional bibliographies help us better conceptualize and visualize trends in Shakespeare scholarship because of their comprehensiveness and attention to specific contexts.

Just as Pujante and Cerdá articulated their vision for the next steps for their bibliography and outlined how these lists can shape the claims we make, reviewers of the bibliography also proposed improvements to the bibliography: many suggested that this work would be more usable were it online. In his positive review, Juan Antonio Pietro Pablos suggests, "A searchable online bibliography would not only make it more accessible to scholars worldwide and facilitate research; it would also grant the opportunity to correct and, if necessary, enlarge it."[159] Pietro Pablos notes that this project already houses an online performance database, *ShakRep: Shakespeare Performance in Spain*, which takes a bibliographical approach, with textual information about performance. Tronch notes that the unannotated version of this bibliography is available on *La Recepción de las Obras de Shakespeare* (um.es/web/shakespeare/), a digital project in which both editors are involved and which offers the bibliography in two PDFs, one ordered chronologically and one ordered alphabetically. These downloads lack Pujante and Cerdá's important introduction and the annotations, as well as the bilingual paratexts (many created, as the copyright page notes, by Keith Gregor) that make this work usable by Spanish and English readers equally. An easy-to-access eBook could be an interim step before turning to a complete database, as it would take a bibliographer time and considerable financial and technical resources to remediate this bibliography.

---

[158] Jesús Tronch, review of *Shakespeare En Espãna: Bibliografia Anotada Bilingue | Shakespeare in Spain: An Annotated Bilingual Bibliography*, eds. Ángel-Luis Pujante and Juan F. Cerdá, *Miscelánea: A Journal of English and American Studies* 54 (2016): 137–69, 161.

[159] Juan Antonio Prieto-Pablos, review of *Shakespeare En Espãna: Bibliografia Anotada Bilingue | Shakespeare in Spain: An Annotated Bilingual Bibliography*, ed. Ángel-Luis Pujante and Juan F. Cerdá, *Atlantis: Journal of the Spanish Association of Anglo-American Studies* 38, no. 4 (2016): 261–5, 264.

Rather than calling for a database, Rayner strikes a different tone in her review:

> Recently, the University of Lisbon's performance database was temporarily out of action whilst I was preparing a chapter on Portuguese performances of Shakespeare. My panic made me realize just how dependent I had become on that database but also made me newly appreciative of the good old technology of the book.[160]

As Rayner points out, an online project is only good if it is available – and we know that no digital project is guaranteed longevity.[161]

Before we turn to how digital publication affects regional bibliographies, let us first briefly consider thematic bibliographies. No discussion of Spanish Shakespeare bibliography could be complete without pointing to one particular Spanish bibliographer: José Ramón Díaz Fernández. Díaz Fernández's work does not usually emphasize Spanish Shakespeare scholarship; rather, his bibliographies are thematic, often focusing on Shakespeare and film.[162] Díaz Fernández's publications offer a fantastic example of how thematic bibliographies support scholarship by showing recent developments in a given area of study. For instance, in 2008, he published "Teen Shakespeare Films: An Annotated Survey of Criticism" in *Shakespeare Bulletin*, focusing on a specific subset of Shakespeare and film.[163] In "*King Lear* on Screen: Select Film-Bibliography," he focused on television, film, and theatrical adaptations of *Lear* and the scholarship about those

---

[160] Rayner, review, 136.

[161] Joanna Tucker, "Facing the Challenge of Digital Sustainability as Humanities Researchers," *Journal of the British Academy* 10 (2022): 93–120.

[162] One exception to this rule is his piece, "Toward a Survey of Shakespeare in Latin America," in *Latin American Shakespeares*, eds. Bernice W. Kliman and Rick J. Santos (Fairleigh Dickinson University Press, 2005), 293–326.

[163] José Ramón Díaz Fernández, "Teen Shakespeare Films: An Annotated Survey of Criticism," *Shakespeare Bulletin* 26, no. 2 (2008): 89–133.

adaptations.[164] And in "Shakespeare on Screen in the Digital Era: An Annotated Bibliography," which appeared in *Cahiers Élisabéthains* in 2021, he focused on publications about Shakespeare from 2002 to 2020.[165] Often included in handbooks on a particular topic, specialized bibliographies like Díaz Fernández's encourage scholars to join larger conversations and acknowledge existing work. Díaz Fernández, like Sasaki in the Japanese context, extends his scholarly generosity by submitting the bibliographies he creates to the *WSB*. These smaller bibliographies are valuable contributions on their own, but they also bring coverage that might otherwise be missed in larger bibliographies. Simply put, although Díaz Fernández is a Spanish Shakespeare bibliographer, his bibliographies are thematically based, with clear ambits that do not focus on a particular language or region, but instead, cluster around specific themes that transcend regional boundaries.

Although bibliographies often cluster around geopolitical nations or regions, they can also be based on culture and language. Dídac Pujol, for instance, has published bibliographies about Shakespeare's translations into Catalan.[166] Pujol traces a history of Catalan Shakespeare bibliography back to the 1930s to reveal a bibliographical tradition that engages with Catalan Shakespeare from the nineteenth century to the present. Pujol evaluates these bibliographies in terms of currency, accuracy, comprehensiveness, and annotations/commentary.[167] By focusing on Shakespeare in Catalonia, Pujol posits that Shakespeare studies in Catalonia are distinct from other related traditions, which itself argues for the cultural and linguistic

---

[164] José Ramón Díaz Fernández, "*King Lear* on Screen: Select Film-Bibliography," in *Shakespeare on Screen: King Lear*, eds. Victoria Bladen, Sarah Hatchuel, and Nathalie Vienne-Guerrin (Cambridge University Press, 2019), 227–47.

[165] José Ramón Díaz Fernández, "Shakespeare on Screen in the Digital Era: An Annotated Bibliography," *Cahiers Élisabéthains* 105, no. 1 (2021): 128–69.

[166] Dídac Pujol, "Bibliografia comentada de les traduccions catalanes de Shakespeare: Part I (1874–1969)," *Estudis Romànics* 32 (2009): 285–308; and "Bibliografia comentada de les traduccions catalanes de Shakespeare: part II (1970–2010)," *Estudis Romànics* 33 (2011): 211–36.

[167] Pujol, "Bibliografia . . . part I," 286.

distinctiveness of Catalonia. Regional Shakespeare bibliographies are political by virtue of the scopes they set. Pujol and other Catalan bibliographers highlight the importance of Shakespeare to Catalonia, while also using their engagement with Shakespeare to show the value of Catalan culture and literature to the rest of the world.

Enumerative bibliography is about listing, but also about numerating, that is, counting. Thus, by listing works on a given topic, or from a given region, a bibliographer says: "These count. These matter." Regional, linguistic, or thematic bibliographies can be individual labors that are shared into larger collaborations, weaving threads of Shakespeare scholarship together.

4.4 Regional Bibliographies and the Digital

As this Element has illustrated so far, early bibliographies emerged from lists. As this subsection will show, these lists and bibliographies are now often moving online. They use database technologies and overlap with databases, but of course, not all databases are bibliographies, nor are all bibliographies databases. A previous rule of thumb to differentiate databases from bibliographies is that databases contain the items they list (and therefore offer incomplete lists) and bibliographies attempt to offer complete lists and do not store the items they include. With evolving technologies and digital crosswalks between platforms, however, that can be hard to disambiguate. (When the *WSB* first introduced direct links to library holdings with the "Get it for me" button, which might be customized by a subscribing institution, the response was wholeheartedly positive, though one subscriber noted that it would now be impossible to teach students the difference between a bibliography and a database.)

The work of gathering regional translations, scholarship, performance, or other material related to Shakespeare lends itself to digital publication. An online interface can also make sharing information easier. Bi-Qi Beatrice Li's special issue of *Early Modern Digital Review* (focusing on Shakespeare in performance) begins with reviews of transnational projects, such as *Global Shakespeares* and *A|S|I|A: The Asian Shakespeare Intercultural Archive* before turning to digital projects that focus on different given regions. As Li writes, "Because of their clear focus on a single locale, these projects suggest a chronological narrative and sustenance historicization, contextualization, and intertextual and influence studies. Their documentation of older productions, many without photos or videos, helps to trace Shakespeare's trajectory, development, and evolution into the present time."[168] Some of these projects attempt a bibliographic approach, that is, documenting everything within their scope. While we do not have space here to rehearse every project discussed in Li's special issue (we encourage you to read the reviews), let alone every digital Shakespeare project that provides bibliographic information, we conclude this section by turning to two different cases that marry bibliographies of performances and bibliographies of secondary sources: *Shakespeare in the Philippines* and the *Canadian Adaptations of Shakespeare Project*.

Shech Pacariem's *Shakespeare in the Philippines* is a website devoted to documenting information about key Filipino Shakespeare performances from 2008 to 2018 with three non-exhaustive bibliographies of research, translations, and reviews.[169] Pacariem created it in order to share in-progress research for graduate school, which explains the site's limited and detailed focus. The project is a strong example of the value of public and open humanities. *Shakespeare in the Philippines* includes links to reviews, publicity, and social media accounts. Yet, as Michaela Atienza's review notes,

> The digital landscape restructures itself constantly. Practically speaking, this means that links cease to function; posts are deleted; social media accounts disappear or are removed from public view. As Pacariem has pointed out,

[168] Bi-Qi Beatrice Li, "Introduction: Special Issue, Digital Representations of Contemporary Shakespeare Performances," *Early Modern Digital Review* 4, no. 1 (2021): 183–8, 187. Li's special issue is also published in *Renaissance and Reformation / Renaissance et Réforme* 44, no. 2 (2021), jps.library.utoronto.ca/index.php/emdr/article/view/37579

[169] Shech Pacariem, *Shakespeare in the Philippines*, archivingshakespeare.wordpress.com.

> tracking the production, marketing, documentation, and reception of Shakespeare becomes even more challenging in such conditions, and researching older performances not documented or promoted using social media becomes more difficult.[170]

As the Internet evolves and links change (even from libraries and archival institutions), it is unclear whether the same online record of these productions will persist for another twenty years. Perhaps not much of what exists now will survive, but at least some relevant information will be preserved in Pacariem's site, if it is still up, of course. And even though major productions should be indexed in the *World Shakespeare Bibliography*, this aggregating resource is created by people with finite resources, and there are always some gaps, particularly in international and non-English coverage.

On a larger scale, the online publication of the *Canadian Adaptations of Shakespeare Project* (*CASP*) announced the importance of Shakespeare in Canada and centered that importance on adaptation. In "Theatrical Adaptations of Shakespeare in Canada: A Working Bibliography," the first iteration of what would become *CASP*, Daniel Fischlin explained the significance of Shakespearean adaptation in Canada as a way of offering a rationale for the project: it is "not only a vastly understudied phenomenon but also a useful index of the myriad ways in which theatrical culture comments on issues of national identity formation."[171] From this bibliography, printed in *Canadian Theatre Review*, grew a comprehensive digital project that included new secondary research, access to full-text scripts, and some multimedia content.[172] Christy Desmet asserts that curation is at the

---

[170] Qtd. in Michaela Atienza, review of "Shakespeare in the Philippines: A Digital Archive of Research and Performance," by Shech Pacariem, *Early Modern Digital Review* 4, no. 2 (2021): 214–18, 216, jps.library.utoronto.ca/index.php/emdr/article/view/37587.

[171] Daniel Fischlin, "Theatrical Adaptations of Shakespeare in Canada: A Working Bibliography," *Canadian Theatre Review* 111 (2002): 67–73, 67.

[172] See Daniel Fischlin, Dorothy Hadfield, Gordon Lester, and Mark A. McCutcheon, "'The Web of Our Life is of a Mingled Yarn': The Canadian

heart of many digital projects about Shakespeare, including *CASP*, noting that "the database and archive [of *CASP*] are, in effect, reliant on the ethos of its creators – their assessment of what is missing and what we need more of – revealing the lingering shadow of the collection at the foundation of the project." Desmet continues, "CASP ... is at heart a collection from an impassioned connoisseur."[173] That is to say, it is the people who create a list who shape its contents. When the focus of a Shakespearean bibliography or list is narrowed, the choices of its creator are even more apparent.

It might seem like the *CASP* bibliography and digital site is a natural choice and, should this project not have been created, a similar one would have to come to be; yet, as the other sections in this volume demonstrate, bibliographers have been more concerned with national projects focusing on one country's scholarly output, an important national Shakespeare library, or production history (consider Cohn's, Kohler's and Wechsung's enumerative contributions to *Shakespeare Jahrbuch* on scholarship, library holdings, and performance, respectively, as comparators). In her 2021 review of *CASP*, Kathryn Prince, a respected scholar in the field of Shakespeare studies in Canada, wrote that the site "will remain a crucial source for anyone working on Canadian and global Shakespeares as long as it is available online."[174] Prince's words foreshadowed the site's demise: *CASP* is now only partially accessible through the Internet Archive's Wayback machine, with the note that "We are working on providing access to the rich trove of scholarship from the CASP site."[175] Despite collaborations from major scholars,

Adaptations of Shakespeare Project, Humanities Scholarship, and ColdFusion," *College Literature* 36, no. 1 (2009): 77–103.

[173] Christy Desmet, "The Art of Curation: Searching for Global Shakespeares in the Digital Archives," *Borrowers and Lenders: The Journal of Shakespeare and Appropriation* 11, no. 1 (2017), borrowers-ojs-azsu.tdl.org/borrowers/article/view/258.

[174] Kathryn Prince, review of "Canadian Adaptations of Shakespeare Project (CASP)," ed. Daniel Fischlin, *Early Modern Digital Review* 4, no. 2 (2021): 2047, 207, jps.library.utoronto.ca/index.php/emdr/article/view/37584.

[175] Daniel Fischlin, www.uoguelph.ca/~dfischli/.

funding from national agencies, and use by the scholarly community, the unfortunate fact remains that this site is, in 2026, not available.

Digital bibliographies and digital projects will not last forever, and none are too big to fail. As with all digital projects, online bibliographies require continued human, institutional, and financial investment to update and maintain. That said, thanks to the collaboration and creativity of scholars and institutions, long-standing Shakespeare bibliographies can continue to exist, even as they evolve into forms unimaginable to their creators. With this in mind, we turn now to the biggest online Shakespeare bibliography, the *World Shakespeare Bibliography*, to see how it got online, how it stays online, the people and decisions that shape it, and how those choices, in turn, shape what we can search.

5 Collaboration and Technology in the *World Shakespeare Bibliography*

Digital technologies have revolutionized bibliography, even though those changes may not always be readily apparent to users of digital bibliographies, who primarily treat bibliographies as instruments to find what they need for their research. In fact, when technology is working smoothly, the tremendous amount of labor behind the forward-facing resource scholars consult in order to do their own work is made practically invisible. While bibliography has long been collaborative, computer technologies have expanded the field of bibliography to include computer programmers as collaborators. In the best case scenarios, programmers work closely with bibliographers to ensure that the digital bibliography is usable and accurate. As the technologies are updated, new technical considerations may arise that need to be addressed to make sure that the version of the site that users see and search functions continue to work correctly. Additionally, digital bibliographies complicate the issue of time. For example, in the days of print bibliographies, updating entries was often difficult. If there was more than one edition of the bibliography, then those items that had been missed in the initial printing had to be added, and any typos or other mistakes in the first edition corrected. However, subsequent editions may not be printed, and as soon as a bibliography is sent to the publisher, it may have already been woefully out-of-date. While a digital bibliography can be updated as new books and articles become available, these updates and corrections are still labor-intensive and require a sustained financial commitment to the resource.

The *World Shakespeare Bibliography* provides us with an interesting case study that illuminates how technology has affected the field of bibliography. One might describe the *WSB* as a very early example of a digital humanities project. In fact, the *WSB*'s editorial staff was using computer technology to produce a bibliography long before the existence of the term "digital humanities."[176] This section describes the history of the *WSB* with a focus on how the editorial staff utilized computers and digital technologies to create a cumulative, annotated bibliography of articles, books, musical scores, films, staged performances, musical recordings, radio broadcasts, multimedia performances, and digital projects about Shakespeare. This historical overview highlights the use of computers and digital technologies at the *WSB* in the following stages: (1) using computers to produce print versions of the *WSB* (complete with an index); (2) using computers to conduct searches; (3) moving a searchable database to a CD-ROM; (4) moving an updated and searchable database online; and (5) refining search capabilities and developing a digital back-end to the project so that the workflow is fully integrated for *WSB* staff and contributors. As this section explores, the *WSB* is a human-created resource that has resulted from generations of collaborative labor and scholarship.

5.1 Computers and Bibliographies: The Early Days, 1976–1985

In 1976, Harrison (Harry) T. Meserole became editor of the *WSB*. The *WSB* editorial offices were at Penn State University, where Meserole was a professor specializing in early American literature and bibliography. Priscilla J. Letterman (later Priscilla J. Letterman Meserole after her marriage to Harry in 2002) had been working as Meserole's assistant since 1965, when

---

[176] On the history of DH as discipline and term, see Matthew Kirschenbaum, "What Is Digital Humanities and What's It Doing in English Departments?" *Association of Departments of English Bulletin* (2010): 1–7.

Meserole was editor of the *MLA International Bibliography* (1957–1975).[177] She was still working with Meserole when the Folger Shakespeare Library contacted him about becoming editor of the *WSB*. Meserole stepped into the role of *WSB* editor, and Letterman Meserole turned her attention to assisting him with producing the *WSB* annually as an issue of *Shakespeare Quarterly*, as discussed in Section 3.

Though Meserole famously avoided working on computers, he recognized that, if the *WSB* was to be a vital bibliography for scholars, it would need to migrate to computers, and he wanted to ensure successful computerization of entries (commonly referred to by those in the *WSB* editorial offices as "records") in the *WSB* database.[178] As Meserole worked to expand the *WSB*'s coverage, he turned his attention to record structure and preparing records for entry into a computerized system.[179] In the *World Shakespeare Bibliography* for 1975, Meserole noted progress in computerizing *WSB* data:

> Entry format is basically that of the *MLA Style Sheet*. To facilitate future storage of data in the computer, however,

---

[177] Priscilla J. Letterman Meserole, telephone conversation with Kris L. May, February 17, 2023. While he was editor of the *MLA International Bibliography*, Meserole oversaw the early process of computerizing bibliographic data. While at Penn State University, Letterman Meserole recalls producing punch cards that were fed into computers to process data for annual volumes of the *MLA International Bibliography*.

[178] James L. Harner, "Harrison T. Meserole: 25 July 1921–20 December 2006: In Memoriam," *Seventeenth-Century News* 65, no. 1–2 (2007): 1–4. Harner recalled Meserole's aversion to computers: "Harry's farsightedness in creating one of the first humanities databases is all the more remarkable since he himself never used a computer. In all the years we shared the same office suite, I recall seeing him touch only *one* computer key *one* time!" (2).

[179] Meserole had been working to computerize the *WSB* as early as the 1970s. *Shakespeare Quarterly* editor John F. Andrews noted, "Commencing with the Bibliography to be published in the Autumn 1977 issue... Professor Meserole expects to employ full computerization, thereby augmenting the efficiency and flexibility with which entries may be recorded and retrieved for scholarly purposes" ("From the Editor," 387).

> certain modifications have been introduced. Every item is
> dated. Arabic numbers have replaced roman to denote the
> volume number of a journal. When the issue number of
> a journal is required for a given entry, it appears in lower-
> case roman immediately after the arabic volume number. An
> arabic number preceded by F in square brackets following
> an entry title refers to an item listed in the "Festschriften and
> Other Analyzed Collections" sub-section which begins the
> Bibliography. An asterisk (*) preceding the author's name of
> an item listed in this Bibliography indicates that the item has
> been entered in previous years' compilations, but is the
> subject of the current reviews or review-articles for which
> data are provided at the end of the entry.[180]

Meserole clearly understood the value of a well-structured record and knew that this structure was key to computerizing bibliographic data. Preparing records to be readable, sortable, and searchable by a computer involves people, though the focus on technology often de-emphasizes (or renders invisible) the intensity of human labor required to make the technology work.

The *WSB* editor had to find a collaborator with the technical knowledge to make the computerization of records a reality. Soon after his appointment as editor of the *WSB* in 1976, Meserole began working with John B. Smith – an English professor who was also a research consultant in Penn State's Computation Center – to produce annual print issues of the *WSB*.[181] The annual cumulation of bibliographical entries was one piece of a project that was to be called the Cumulative Shakespeare Bibliography: a computerized "bibliographic database of Shakespeare scholarship and dramatic

---

[180] Meserole, "Shakespeare: Annotated World Bibliography for 1975," 389–498, 389–90.

[181] Smith's duties while at Penn State included promoting the use of computers to faculty and students in the humanities (John B. Smith, telephone conversation with Kris L. May, August 9, 2023).

productions."[182] Part 1 of the project was to produce a bibliography that contained records from 1958 to 1979, and Part 2 of the project, which was initially funded by the National Endowment for the Humanities, was to extend the database to include entries from as far back as 1900.[183] The Cumulative Shakespeare Bibliography would be available in three forms: a conventionally published, inclusive reference work; current year cumulations published in *Shakespeare Quarterly*; and computer printouts of specific search requests offered through a custom retrieval service.[184] Of all of these, the annual bibliography was the only piece that was actually produced. Nevertheless, the Cumulative Shakespeare Bibliography project did result in the hierarchical taxonomic encoding system that the *WSB* editorial staff would use in some form until the system was rebuilt in 2016. Additionally, the Cumulative Shakespeare Bibliography also provided Boolean search functionality of the data, which meant that the editorial staff could search the growing database.[185]

When Smith arrived on the scene, the *WSB* offices were already a hub of activity. Letterman Meserole oversaw the day-to-day administrative functioning of the office on the Penn State campus, which included keeping track of all of the items received in the mail. The scope of the *WSB* was international, which meant not all books and articles were readily available at the university's library. The *WSB* offices received photocopies of books and articles retrieved through Interlibrary Loan, as well as books from publishers and correspondents all over the world. The daily work of creating the bibliography was (and remains), therefore, collaborative.

---

[182] Harrison T. Meserole and John B. Smith, "'Yet There Is Method in It': The Cumulative Shakespeare Bibliography—A Product of Project Planning in the Humanities," *Perspectives in Computing* 1, no. 2 (1981): 4-11, 4.

[183] "Harner Named Editor of World Shakespeare Bibliography," *The Shakespeare Newsletter* 43, no. 217 (1993): 35.

[184] Meserole and Smith, "'Yet There Is Method in It,'" 4.

[185] Meserole and Smith estimated that the entire database of the Cumulative Shakespeare Bibliography, 1900–1979, would contain "approximately 100,000 categorized, annotated, and verified citations from more than 40 countries" ("'Yet There Is Method in It,'" 4).

Graduate students were constantly in the office to collect index cards from Meserole that would include bibliographic information about items to be added to the bibliography. They would then retrieve books and articles from the library stacks and bring them to the *WSB* offices. Annotations were then composed – on index cards – by Meserole and the graduate students.[186]

Editors began using computers in the production of the *WSB* as the bibliography was transitioning to photo-offset printing. Smith's computer code was primarily driving the photo-offset process.[187] Before offset printing, *WSB* editors would deliver final typewritten manuscripts to the printer, who would set the type on each page, manually laying out the pages for publication. With offset printing, the printer used a photocomposer machine to enter and format text. Offset printing streamlined the creation of the annual bibliography and reduced overall printing costs by using a computerized system to convert an electronic bibliographic file into an electronic file that included photocomposer protocol tags.[188]

Working closely with Meserole, Smith developed a system of programs called BAG/2 – "A Bibliographic and Grouping System for Natural Language Data" – to handle bibliographical citations.[189] The *WSB* editorial

---

[186] Smith, telephone conversation. [187] Smith, telephone conversation.

[188] The savings in printing costs were significant. As Meserole and Smith noted in 1981, "to produce a page of camera-ready copy for the cumulative bibliography would cost about $40 for typesetting manuscripts in typescript, compared with $7 for 'manuscripts' coded on magnetic tape." This translated to an overall savings of almost $80,000 for printing a reference work of approximately 2,300 pages of entries dated between 1958 and 1979 ("'Yet There Is Method in It,'" 7).

[189] John B. Smith, "BAG/2: A Bibliographic and Grouping System for Natural Language Data" (Pennsylvania State University Computation Center, November 1981). BAG/2 included five programs written in PL/I, as well as some IBM utilities: three of the programs would "SCAN the data, SORT them, and [...] TRANSFER the sorted data to the MASTER file; two are used to SEARCH and extract from the data base [sic] the information requested, and to INDEX the data base [sic]." Though BAG/2 was created specifically for using with bibliographies, it was also "suitable for any data base [sic] that structurally resembles a bibliography – that is, a collection of individual records consisting of

History of Shakespearean Bibliography 79

staff created the bibliography using BAG/2, which included taxonomic codes for both subject and form.[190] In a nutshell, the first line of each bibliographic record served as a "subject taxonomic marker," which was used "hierarchically to divide the data base [sic] into separately ordered and extractable sections."[191] Additionally, identifiable fields within each bibliographical record were "marked with a form taxonomy marker," which "would designate: author, title, journal, date of publication, descriptor terms, etc."[192] The bespoke coding system looked like this: each line of the record began with a "%," and the two-digit numeral following the period indicated what kind of data was contained within the field.[193] For example:

%.10 Author, index form
%.15 Author, substitute print form
%.20 Title, separately published
%.25 Title, contained
%.30 Imprint statement
%.35 Date (suppressed)
%.40 Annotation
%.50 Reviews
%.61 Names for index
%.64 Descriptive terms for index
%.80 Accession number

identifiable components (author, title, etc.) ordered alphabetically under a subject taxonomic scheme (e.g., algebra, analysis, . . ., topology)" (Smith, "BAG/2," 1).

[190] John B. Smith, email message to Kris L. May, August 11, 2023.

[191] Smith, "BAG/2," 10. The subject taxonomic marker was the percent-sign character (%) followed by two-digit categories and separated by periods. For example, "%30.14.05.05" indicated the record was about the individual work *Hamlet* (%30.14), was a work of criticism and scholarship (.05), and was a bibliography or checklist (.05) (Smith, "BAG/2," 10–11).

[192] Smith, "BAG/2," 11. [193] Smith, "BAG/2," 12.

Each entry, complete with taxonomic codes, was entered into the computer mainframe system at Penn State.[194]

In consultation with a contact in the photocomposer shop, Smith wrote a program to take out the BAG/2 tags and insert photocomposer tags so that the text and formatting would transfer accurately. The print shop received the electronic files on a computer tape, which included the data marked with photocomposer tags. The tagged data file was put into the photocomposer, which generated camera-ready copies of the pages. The printed pages were sent to the editorial staff for proofreading, and the shop person would manually enter changes into the photocomposer. Finally, the print shop used the photocomposer system to adjust final spacing and ensure the best layout and proper page breaks.[195]

This collaboration between bibliographer and computer programmer offers insights into the push-and-pull between Meserole's desire to ensure adherence to strict bibliographic standards and Smith's attempts to simplify the process of computerization so that the system could be as efficient and flexible as possible. Meserole and Smith agreed that, ultimately, what they were designing would need to be usable by scholars and students.[196] If the system was too difficult or cumbersome, then it would not be used. With this in mind, they put together an advisory committee of "eight senior scholars" to help them design a system that would be simple enough for humanities students and scholars to use and to explain to their colleagues, thus "building the support in the scholarly community necessary to ensure the bibliography's acceptance... [and] utility."[197] The advisory group was

---

[194] Smith, telephone conversation.

[195] Smith, email message. As Smith recalls, the electronic files on the computer tape did not include coding to break the continuous series of bibliographic records into pages. Final page breaks and other spacing issues would have been part of the final steps in the process and performed by the printer's system based on the spacing generated by the characters and fonts.

[196] Meserole and Smith, "'Yet There Is Method in It,'" 5–6.

[197] Meserole and Smith, "'Yet There Is Method in It,'" 6. The scholars who served on the advisory committee for the Cumulative Shakespeare Bibliography were John F. Andrews (Folger Shakespeare Library), David Bevington (University of Chicago), Maurice Charney (Rutgers University), Alan C. Dessen

also particularly helpful in the development of the taxonomic system, as they thought through "what information to embed in the taxonomy and what to include in the data record itself."[198]

Not surprisingly, Meserole and Smith had to negotiate many details of the records. For example, in the 1960s, 1970s, and 1980s, it was common for Eastern European authors of play reviews to sign their names with lowercase initials (e.g., r. k.). When the index sorted names, these initials would appear as the very first items in the name index (k., r.) before those last names beginning with uppercase *A*. Instead of "modify[ing] the standard SORT package or develop[ing] a seldom-used separate SORT field," Meserole and Smith decided to let the lowercase initial names appear at the beginning of the index, even though this was not the standard practice for indexing a print bibliography: "score one for efficiency."[199] Another challenge presented itself when it came to indexing the names of multi-authored works. The name index dictated that all names in the index should appear as Last_Name, First_Name Middle_Name. However, bibliographic standards also required that only the name of the first author appear this way in a citation. All other authors' names appear in Anglo-centric "normal order" (First_Name Middle_Name Last_Name). Even though the *WSB* was international in scope, the editors made a decision to impose Anglo-centric order on names, despite non-Western names often not following this logic. Meserole and Smith decided to keep the names of subsequent authors in multiauthored works in "normal order" for the bibliographic record and to index the name according to established bibliographic practice, with last name first, even though it required multiple pages of closely written PL/I code: "score one for tradition."[200]

(University of North Carolina), Roland Mushat Frye (University of Pennsylvania), Michael Kiernan (The Pennsylvania State University), Marvin Rosenberg (University of California, Berkeley), and Susan Snyder (Swarthmore College) (Meserole and Smith, "'Yet There Is Method in It,'" 11).

[198] Meserole and Smith, "'Yet There Is Method in It,'" 6.

[199] Meserole and Smith, "'Yet There Is Method in It,'" 8.

[200] Meserole and Smith, "'Yet There Is Method in It,'" 8.

From 1979 to 1983, *Shakespeare Quarterly* listed both Meserole and Smith as editors on the first page of each volume: "Edited by HARRISON T. MESEROLE [and] JOHN B. SMITH."[201] The biographical footnotes on those same pages describe Smith as "Technical Editor for the World Shakespeare Bibliography."[202] Smith was the first Technical Editor at the *WSB*, indicating the significance of a computer programmer to the bibliographical project.

Though the Cumulative Shakespeare Bibliography never culminated in the initially envisioned publication of a reference book or record-retrieval service that would deliver specific search requests via a computer printout, the project did result in the computerization of records for an annual bibliography published in *Shakespeare Quarterly*. Shortly after beginning to computerize records, Meserole and the *WSB* moved from Penn State to the Department of English at Texas A&M University, where *WSB* editors and staff continued refining the computerization process. Well aware of the amount of work involved in producing the *WSB* annually – and perhaps

[201] Harrison T. Meserole and John B. Smith, "Shakespeare: Annotated World Bibliography for 1978," *Shakespeare Quarterly* 30, no. 4 (1979): 454–635, 454; Meserole and Smith, "Shakespeare Annotated World Bibliography for 1979," *Shakespeare Quarterly* 31, no. 4 (1980): 468–659, 468; Meserole and Smith, "Shakespeare: Annotated Bibliography for 1980," *Shakespeare Quarterly* 32, no. 4 (1981): 420–684, 420; Meserole and Smith, "Shakespeare: Annotated World Bibliography for 1981," *Shakespeare Quarterly* 33, no. 5 (1982): 548–804, 548; and Meserole and Smith, "Shakespeare: Annotated World Bibliography for 1982," *Shakespeare Quarterly* 33, no. 5 (1983): 516–784, 516.

[202] Meserole and Smith, "Shakespeare: Annotated World Bibliography for 1978," 454; Meserole and Smith, "Shakespeare Annotated World Bibliography for 1979," 468; Meserole and Smith, "Shakespeare: Annotated Bibliography for 1980," 420; Meserole and Smith, "Shakespeare: Annotated World Bibliography for 1981," 548; Meserole and Smith, "Shakespeare: Annotated World Bibliography for 1982," 516. The frontmatter of "Shakespeare Annotated World Bibliography for 1978" thanks Timothy K. Conley, Priscilla J. Letterman Meserole, and John B. Smith, "who assumed major responsibility for preparing final copy of the Bibliography for the press during the Editor's illness" (457).

also acknowledging the amount of work still needed to computerize the *WSB* – Meserole insisted that Texas A&M also hire and move Letterman Meserole (along with Harry's prize-winning orchids and greenhouse) to Texas so that the two could continue collaborating on the *WSB*. The negotiations were successful, and Meserole, Letterman Meserole, and the *WSB* moved to Texas A&M in 1985.[203]

5.2 CD-ROM and the World Wide Web, 1986–1999

As Meserole began to think about the future of the *WSB* beyond his editorship and who might be the best editor to guide the bibliography's continued computerization, he approached James L. Harner, who was then at Bowling Green State University, about moving to Texas A&M and becoming the next editor of the *WSB* in early 1988. Later that year, Harner and his family moved to Texas, and Harner began working in the Department of English at Texas A&M University with the understanding that, when Meserole stepped down as editor of the *WSB*, Harner would become the next editor. Meserole and Harner began working together on the *WSB* as soon as Harner arrived at Texas A&M and continued to share editorial responsibilities until Meserole stepped down as editor in 1992.[204]

When Harner arrived at Texas A&M, the computerization of *WSB* records that had started at Penn State was well underway. Through Texas A&M's IT Department, Meserole connected with Roger Sorrells, a computer programmer interested in Shakespeare and the digitization of the *WSB*'s bibliographic entries. Harner, Letterman Meserole, and Sorrells refined the text-entry template for word processing, which the *WSB* editorial staff would work with in some shape or form until the relaunching of the *WSB*'s website in 2016. Letterman Meserole shifted her focus exclusively to proofreading, while Harner and Sorrells ironed out the computerization details on Texas A&M's mainframe computer system. The *WSB* staff – which included a group of graduate research assistants in the Department of English at Texas A&M – entered data into the

[203] Letterman Meserole, telephone conversation.

[204] Darinda Harner, telephone conversation with Kris L. May, December 21, 2022.

template that would ultimately facilitate the transformation of information prepared for a print issue of *Shakespeare Quarterly* into digital format.[205]

In the 1980s and 1990s, CD-ROM databases significantly altered the landscape for researchers accustomed to using printed bibliographies to discover and locate sources. CD-ROM technology was an important early step into a world where scholars would no longer have to shuffle their way through print-only issues of bibliographies (which may or may not be on their university library's shelves) to track down sources for articles, papers, and lectures. With its adoption of CD-ROM technology, the *WSB* paralleled *The MLA International Bibliography*, *The Oxford English Dictionary (OED)*, and *The Annual Bibliography of English Language and Literature (ABELL)*, all of which underwent digitization in the 1980s and 1990s. Together, these histories of digitization demonstrate both how the initial adoption of CD-ROM technology marked a paradigm shift in how bibliographic and reference materials were compiled, edited, and accessed, and how the *World Shakespeare Bibliography*, despite its small staff and limited resources, was an early adopter of the technologies that undergird digital bibliographic projects to this day.

Both the *MLA International Bibliography* and the *Oxford English Dictionary* adopted CD-ROM technology in 1987 to much applause, while the *Annual Bibliography of English Language and Literature* developed a web presence in 1993 and expanded to CD-ROM in 1998. In her 1986 Report, MLA Executive Director Phyllis Franklin highlighted the transformational impact of the MLA's upcoming adoption of the compact disc: "the MLA's entire Bibliography from 1921 through the present – six feet of bookshelf space – can be stored on a single disc."[206] The *Oxford English Dictionary* similarly lauded its new CD-ROM technology as "a great contrast to the hefty twenty-volume work that took up four feet of shelf space and weighed

---

[205] Letterman Meserole, telephone conversation.

[206] "History of the *MLA International Bibliography*: A Timeline" *The Modern Language Association* (accessed October 17, 2025), cdn.knightlab.com/libs/timeline3/latest/embed/index.html?source=1q3yTHPJjmhqD0Sk4zxxwbjdlr6kXgo47UKXvmG1FbBI.

150 pounds!"[207] While the promise of freed-up bookshelves likely pleased some users, the MLA and *OED*'s enthusiastic celebrations of the space-saving capabilities of CDs also convey how the digitization of these resources fundamentally changed the way scholars undertook research. From the comfort of their computer terminals, researchers could access and search hundreds of years of scholarship without ever having to pull a heavy tome or crumbling journal from the shelves. But the adoption of new technologies – as we have seen before – also ushers in the need for new and different types of labor. Foregrounding the expertise and knowledge required to bring *ABELL* onto the World Wide Web and CD-ROM, *ABELL* editor Gerard Lowe thanks Cambridge University Library's "Automation Department" and "IT Services" for "help and advice in this venture" in the prefaces to the Annual Bibliographies of 1993 and 1994.[208] The introduction of new types of labor into the preparation and presentation of digital bibliographic and reference materials, paired with the nimbleness with which these resources pivoted from "the era of index cards and paper clips" to "new software which revolutionized" bibliographic practices, demonstrates, once more, the push and pull of technological advancements that make bibliographies easier for researchers to use and that can also make more work for bibliographic teams.[209]

Like those who heralded the MLA and *OED*'s adoption of CD-ROM technology, reviewers noted how *The World Shakespeare Bibliography on CD-ROM* (hereafter *WSB on CD-ROM*) saved space and transformed how scholars conducted research. In his 1996 review, Hardy Cook notes that four years of *WSB* data "fits on one CD-ROM, while the four print volumes that it constitutes take up three inches of space on the shelf."[210] This

---

[207] "History of the OED," *Oxford English Dictionary*, accessed November 13, 2023, www.oed.com/information/about-the-oed/history-of-the-oed/.

[208] Gerard Lowe, "Preface," *Annual Bibliography of English Language and Literature for 1993* 68 (1995): v; Lowe, "Preface," *Annual Bibliography of English Language and Literature for 1994* 69 (1996): v.

[209] Jennifer Fellow, "Preface," *Annual Bibliography of English Language and Literature for 2001* 76 (2002): v.

[210] Hardy Cook, review of *The World Shakespeare Bibliography on CD-ROM*, ed. James L. Harner, *The Shakespeare Newsletter* 46, no. 229 (1996): 33–4, 33.

consolidation of data into one, easily searchable source, Cook explains, also radically changed the amount of time required to perform discrete research tasks: "By using the keyword, proximity, and boolean search capabilities of the CD-ROM, one can identify in moments studies that would by contrast require skimming through complete volumes of print bibliographies."[211]

Other reviews of the *WSB on CD-ROM* echo these sentiments; scholars recognized the paradigm shift in research that they were experiencing firsthand. In his review, Christopher Smith even goes so far as to compare the adoption of CD-ROM technology to the cultural shift ushered in by the invention of the printing press: "In what one day may well come to be dubbed the incunabula age of electronic information retrieval, the development of the greatly respected bibliography regularly published in the *Shakespeare Quarterly* into a CD-ROM, the *World Shakespeare Bibliography* is an event in literary scholarship that merits a report and a review as well as a welcome."[212] Christa Jansohn's review, while not quite ascribing the CD-ROM Gutenbergian status, emphasizes how the digitization of print resources was changing the nature of research. She opens her review with a reflection on how technologies were changing so quickly that soon students and scholars would not even be able to understand that bibliographies had no technical aids and instead depended on flipping through large volumes of printed material (although she did not anticipate the time when the CD-ROM itself would become a forgotten relic).[213] Stacey Stewart's review critiques digital bibliography's learning curve, stating that the *WSB* "is a fine resource if you are willing to invest the time to learn how to use the technology" but that "it's probably not worth the investment" until "the disk covers at least half of the twentieth century."[214] She does, however,

[211] Cook, review, 34.

[212] Christopher Smith, review of *The World Shakespeare Bibliography, 1990–1993 on CD-ROM*, *Shakespeare Yearbook* 8 (1997): 496–9, 496.

[213] Christa Jansohn, review of *The World Shakespeare Bibliography on CD-ROM: 1990–1993*, *Archiv für das Studium der neueren Sprachen und Literaturen* 234, no. 1 (1997): 224–5.

[214] Stacey A. Stewart, review of *The World Shakespeare Bibliography on CD-ROM 1990–1993*, ed. James L. Harner, *Theatre Studies* 42 (1997): 85–6, 86.

celebrate the convenience of the CD. Comparing the "task of sifting through tome after tome of printed matter" with the research capabilities of the CD, Stewart, perhaps a bit cheekily, declares, "the researcher clicks three times and voila! – instant access to an enormous variety of Shakespearean resources."[215] The vast results yielded by a seemingly instantaneous digital search result not only from the labors of the researcher, who "invests" time in mastering bibliographies' technologies, but also from the programmers and bibliographers who built them in the first place. The speed and ease of the digital technology make it easy to overlook its material construction (particularly when the resources function properly), but it is the product of diligent collaborative work.

The *WSB on CD-ROM*, first published in 1996 by Cambridge University Press in association with the Folger Shakespeare Library, covered the years 1990–1993 (Figure 7). It included coverage of "more than 12,000 works published or produced during 1990–1993 (as well as several thousand additional reviews of books, productions, films, and audio recordings)."[216] This initial release package included both the CD-ROM and a fifty-page instruction booklet detailing the scope of the bibliography and explaining how to install the disc, how to perform basic and advanced searches, and how to annotate and print text from entries. Successive versions of the CD-ROM contained the instruction booklet as a DynaText book file preloaded on the CDs. As the promotional pamphlet advertised, "This is not 'technology for technology's sake.' We are not interested in electronic gimmickry or vast amounts of unmarshalled data: our CD-ROMs carry a responsibility to enhance in new ways, to the highest possible standards, the study of the subjects they represent."[217]

The CD-ROMs for the *OED*, the *MLA International Bibliography*, *ABELL*, and the *WSB* reveal how the adoption of digital technologies ushered in new rhythms of publication and altered the temporal landscape

---

[215] Stewart, review, 85.

[216] Harner, *The World Shakespeare Bibliography on CD-ROM, 1990–1993* instruction booklet (Cambridge University Press, 1996), 6.

[217] *CD-ROMs from Cambridge University Press, 1996 Releases*, promotional pamphlet (Cambridge University Press, 1996).

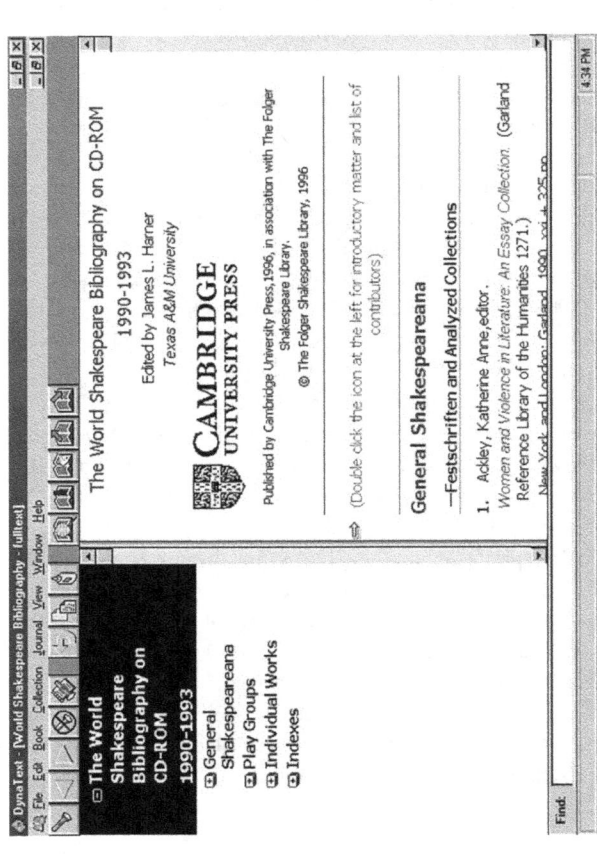

Figure 7 Screenshot of CD-ROM "opening text screen," *World Shakespeare Bibliography on CD-ROM, 1990–1993.*

of many previously annual or periodical publications (as we saw in Section 2 of this Element). As bibliographies and other reference sources began to split between printed and digital editions, and then shifted exclusively to digital, the notion of annual updates (which were often delayed by multiple years) faded into the background as users expected bibliographies and other reference tools to be updated around the clock and to contain the most up-to-date information possible.

Despite the allure of these new digital technologies, their adoption was not easy or straightforward, even for an editorial team that strived to incorporate computers into the creation and digitization of the *WSB* from as early as the 1970s. While no one who worked directly with the *WSB* in the 1980s and 1990s has been able to verify these details, Franklin J. Hildy provides an account of the challenges that the *WSB* encountered on its quest for digitization. Considering that Hildy incorrectly identifies James L. Harner as "James T. Harner" throughout his review of the CD-ROM, one should perhaps take Hildy's presentation of *WSB* inside knowledge with a grain of salt:

> Over the years the bibliography's coverage has grown and so has the Shakespeare industry with which it has been attempting to keep up. The exponential growth has made it a prime candidate for conversion to digital technology and under the leadership of its former editor Harrison T. Meserole of Texas A&M University, attempts were made as early as 1988 to begin the daunting process of of converting the "World Shakespeare Bibliography" to CD-Rom format. The current editor, James T. [sic] Harner, has continued this process but it was not until the bibliography's sponsors, the Folger Shakespeare Library, teamed up with Cambridge University Press in 1996 that the first CD-ROM (covering the years 1990-1993) came to market.[218]

[218] Franklin J. Hildy, review of *The World Shakespeare Bibliography on CD-ROM, 1983–1995*, ed. James [L.] Harner, *Theatre Review* 51, no. 4 (1999): 480–1.

While some of the details of Hildy's review cannot be verified, he correctly identifies the bibliographers' almost incessant urge to grow their bibliographies bigger, better, and more advanced at every turn. When the *WSB* first moved to CD-ROM in 1996, the plan was for the *WSB* to be updated annually, with each successive CD-ROM moving coverage forward one year and backward three years. The first CD-ROM, released in 1996, covered materials from 1990 to 1993; the second CD-ROM, released in 1997, thus extended coverage backward to 1987 and forward to 1994. Highlighting the way in which CD-ROM technology expedited the electronic publication of past print publications, the CD-ROM box for the *WSB on CD-ROM, 1987–1994* reports, "in this second release, coverage is doubled."[219] Pamphlets from Cambridge University advertising the *WSB on CD-ROM* state that the annual updates would continue to extend forward and backward until "the period 1900 to the present day is contained on one disk."[220] As is frequently the case, the desires of the bibliographers, strapped for time and resources, could not be fully met.

Having provided an overview of the digital landscape and the *WSB on CD-ROM*'s impact on this landscape, this section will now turn to the technical specifications of the CD to illustrate how the CD managed to keep some aspects of the print bibliography intact while also introducing fundamentally new ways to use it. The *WSB on CD-ROM, 1990–1993* (released in 1996) and subsequent releases in 1997, 1998, and 1999 were presented as DynaText electronic books.[221] DynaText made it possible to build an electronic bibliography that made use of the same taxonomy that structured

---

[219] Harner, *The World Shakespeare Bibliography on CD-ROM, 1987–1994* (Cambridge University Press, 1997).

[220] *CD-ROMs from Cambridge University Press, 1996 Releases,* promotional pamphlet, 1996.

[221] DynaText, developed by Electronic Book Technologies, Inc. (EBT), was an electronic book publishing system that offered a compiler and indexer with which a publisher could build an electronic book and a browser that enabled readers to navigate, read, and even search the book. At the heart of DynaText's functionality as a system in which electronic books could be both built and accessed was Standard Generalized Markup Language (SGML), a declarative language, that allowed for a plain text document to be tagged or marked up with specific

the print *Bibliography*, that presented individual entries in a way that was nearly identical in appearance to entries in print editions of the *Bibliography*, and that added completely new features such as extensive cross-referencing via hyperlinks and search features that made use of tags (Figure 8). With the adoption of CD-ROM technology that presented the *Bibliography* as an electronic book, the *WSB* was able to provide continuity for long-time users who had become accustomed to its structure in *Shakespeare Quarterly* while also introducing groundbreaking features that, once again, rewrote the rules of bibliographic research.

In a section of the booklet about "Differences between the print and CD-ROM publications," Harner lays out some of the primary ways in which the CD-ROM's functionality differed from that of the annual printed bibliographies in *Shakespeare Quarterly*:

> While *The World Shakespeare Bibliography on CD-ROM* cumulates and significantly expands the annual bibliographies in *Shakespeare Quarterly*, it omits several entries in the latter (especially works peripherally related to Shakespeare, most obituaries of performers, abstracts of unpublished convention papers, and operas not based on Shakespeare texts), condenses some (especially by omitting non-speaking roles in entries for productions), and conflates others (especially abstracts of published works and book or production reviews originally listed as separate entries).[222]

In this way, the adoption of CD-ROM technology allowed for simultaneous expansion and refinement of the material contained in the bibliography, a form of editing of the bibliography that was not available when it was only distributed in print. In short, the CD-ROM allowed for changes to past entries, unlike periodical print publication.

---

vocabulary; see MacKenzie Smith, review of DynaText: An Electronic Publishing System, *Computer and the Humanities* 27, no. 5/6 (1993/1994): 415–20.

[222] Harner, *The World Shakespeare Bibliography on CD-ROM, 1990–1993* instruction booklet, 5.

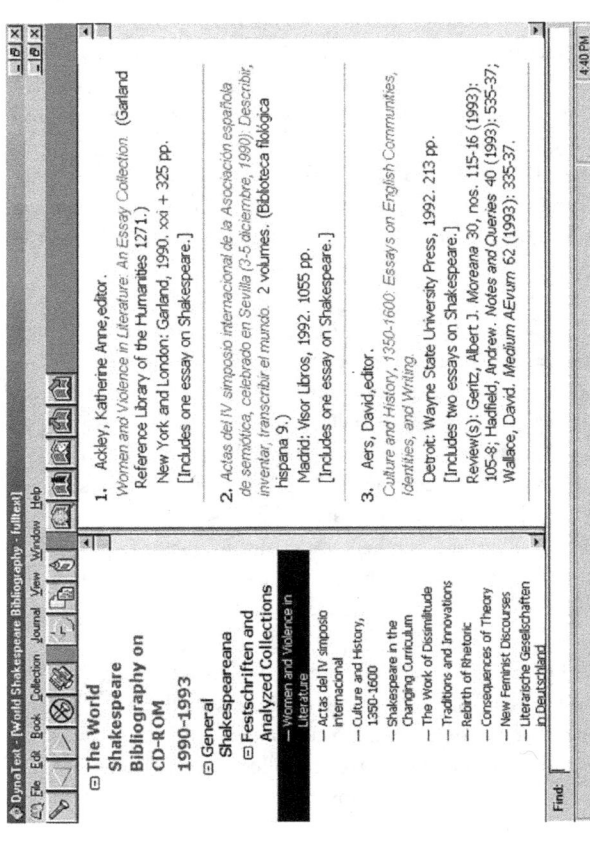

Figure 8 Screenshot of CD-ROM "browse text screen" *World Shakespeare Bibliography on CD-ROM 1990–1993*.

Of special import was the CD-ROM's functionality to present cross-references as hypertext links and to expand on the printed volume's cross-reference functionality through a "See also" icon that "directs readers of an entry to other entries judged relevant by the *Bibliography* editor."[223] In print, cross-references were just as tedious for bibliographers to create as they were tiresome for users to follow. Surprisingly, the "Differences between the print and CD-ROM publication" section of the booklet does not emphasize the search feature available in the electronic book. Today we might take the ability to search electronic resources for granted. In the 1990s, this was revolutionary, but not yet understood well enough to be highlighted as such. One especially useful feature of the simple search is that the number of "hits" for any search term is expressed both in the total occurrence of the search term in the text and in a breakdown of hits for each of the four major divisions that comprise the *WSB*'s taxonomy. For instance, in the *WSB on CD-ROM, 1990–1993*, a simple search of the term "Olivier" provided seventy-seven results. Users of the CD-ROM could see in the table of contents window that these results were broken down by section, such that twelve were in "General Shakespeareana," fifty-two in the "Individual Works," and thirteen in the "Indexes." Though CD-ROM publication of the *WSB* was relatively short-lived, it was a significant step in moving the *WSB* from print to digital. The CD-ROM version allowed for tagging and cross-references, as the *WSB*'s editorial team continued to refine presentation of material to users via a content-rich, interactive, digital interface.

5.3 The End of the Printed World Shakespeare Bibliography *and the* World Shakespeare Bibliography Online, *2001–2013*

In 2001, the *WSB* made its renewed debut on the web as the *World Shakespeare Bibliography Online* – for which it won the prestigious Besterman/McColvin Medal, awarded by the Library Association (London), now the Council of Library and Information Professionals.

---

[223] Harner, *The World Shakespeare Bibliography on CD-ROM, 1990–1993* instruction booklet, 10.

The *WSB* continued to be published as a print issue of *Shakespeare Quarterly* until 2003, when it moved to being published exclusively online by Johns Hopkins University Press (JHUP) and updated quarterly by the *WSB* editorial staff. The final print version was published as "World Shakespeare Bibliography 2003," which appeared as volume 55.5 of *Shakespeare Quarterly* in 2004.[224] An editorial note in the previous volume of *Shakespeare Quarterly* explained that the next-to-last printed edition of the *WSB* was "more than six hundred entries shorter" than the previous year's *WSB*. However, rather than "a reduction in the number of publications about Shakespeare," the decrease in size was due to the "decision to list entries for productions, audio and video recordings, and films only in the *World Shakespeare Bibliography Online*" and not on pages of the printed issue.[225] Furthermore, the final print issue of the *WSB* in 2004 was to be even shorter, as it would exclude the same taxonomic entries that only appeared online the previous year, as well as "reviews of books that were listed in earlier editions of the *WSB*."[226] Harner's editorial note in the final print edition explains that "discontinuing the annual print edition will allow the *Bibliography* staff to improve the coverage and accuracy of the award-winning *World Shakespeare Bibliography Online*."[227] Moving the *WSB* completely online "offer[s] researchers a resource that fully meets their needs and best reflects *Shakespeare Quarterly*'s commitment to maintaining a definitive record of Shakespeare scholarship and productions worldwide."[228]

---

[224] Harner and Kris L. May, "World Shakespeare Bibliography 2003," *Shakespeare Quarterly* 55, no. 5 (2004): 515–785.

[225] Harner, "World Shakespeare Bibliography 2002," *Shakespeare Quarterly* 54, no. 5 (2003): 487–772, 488.

[226] Harner, "World Shakespeare Bibliography 2002," 488. Prior to the *World Shakespeare Bibliography* for 2003, print editions had included book reviews published throughout the year, even if the books under review were published in previous years.

[227] Harner and May, "World Shakespeare Bibliography 2003," 514.

[228] Harner and May, "World Shakespeare Bibliography 2003," 514.

As the print editions of the *WSB* were winding down, Priscilla J. Letterman Meserole was planning her retirement from Texas A&M and the *WSB*. Notably, in the *WSB* for 1992, Letterman Meserole's name appeared for the first time on the title page of the print version of the *WSB* as one of three editors: "James L. Harner, Editor, Harrison T. Meserole, Editor Emeritus," and "Priscilla J. Letterman, Technical Editor."[229] From this point until her retirement, Letterman Meserole was credited as an editor and featured on the title page of the print *WSB* (and in the booklet for the CD-ROM), with other editors. "World Shakespeare Bibliography 2001" (*Shakespeare Quarterly* 53.5, published in 2002) was Letterman Meserole's final issue of the *WSB*, and in honor of her many years of service to the *WSB*, Harner dedicated the issue to Letterman Meserole and personalized the issue by selecting a photo of one of her needlepoint creations to grace the cover of her final issue.[230] By foregrounding the outgoing technical editor's contributions to the *WSB* and including an image of her needlepoint on the cover, Harner acknowledged the labor of his long-time colleague in a way that personalizes one of the final print issues of the *WSB* (Figure 9). Kris L. May was hired a few months before Letterman Meserole retired, so that the outgoing technical editor could train the new technical editor.

One of the labor challenges facing the *WSB*'s move to digital involved the treatment of older entries. Harner and the *WSB* staff planned to post current entries, as well as previous years' entries that had been processed and were ready for digitization. When entries for as far back as 1960 had been processed and moved online, it became apparent that, given the limitations of staff resources, it was in the best interest of the *WSB*'s users

---

[229] James L. Harner, Harrison T. Meserole, and Priscilla J. Letterman, "World Shakespeare Bibliography 1992," *Shakespeare Quarterly* 44, no. 5 (1993): 519–930, 519.

[230] Harner and Letterman, "World Shakespeare Bibliography 2001," *Shakespeare Quarterly* 53, no. 5 (2002): 625–1020. A note on the issue's title page highlights the connection between the needlepoint and the daily operations of the *WSB*: "This piece adorned the walls of the *World Shakespeare Bibliography* office during her tenure as Technical Editor" (625).

Figure 9 Cover of *Shakespeare Quarterly*, 53, no. 5 (2002). Needlepoint by Priscilla J. Letterman Meserole, published by permission.

for the editorial staff to focus on keeping the *WSB* up-to-date with current scholarship and resources and, thus, to discontinue processing entries prior to 1960 for digitization.

As the *WSB* fully transitioned to an online project, Harner also decided to change the "technical editor" job title to "associate editor."

From a practical standpoint, "associate editor" was a preexisting job title at Texas A&M University that better aligned with the duties of the *WSB*'s technical editor. Additionally, as the *WSB* moved from a print publication to an electronic database that was updated quarterly, Harner believed that the associate editor title more accurately represented the duties of the position, which now included not only proofreading text but also composing entries for stage productions, films, radio productions, and television programs and checking and correcting cross-references and online links. Shortly after the final printed edition was published, the *WSB*'s technical editor became the associate editor.

The look and processes of the *WSB* developed in 2001, indeed, the coding systems first developed by Smith and Meserole in 1981, remained much the same for fifteen years. Roger Sorrells, the computer programmer who started working closely with Harner when he arrived at Texas A&M, developed some programs to facilitate the processing of the data files for posting online. Significantly, the actual XML coding for the website was not done in the *WSB* editorial offices. Instead, each quarter, the *WSB* editorial offices would upload processed files to JHUP's website. A JHUP programmer developed an error program to detect duplicates and flag other anomalies in the data. *WSB* editors would review the error files and make necessary corrections. Finally, a programmer at JHUP would run a conversion program that would transform the new data into XML, and the update was posted to the website.

5.4 *Rebuilding the* World Shakespeare Bibliography, *2013–2016*

For many years, the *WSB* continued this inefficient system of processing bibliographic records, which would finally end up being posted online. *WSB* editors never touched the website: the editorial staff would send many processed files to a programmer at JHUP, who would then prepare the data to be uploaded to the XML website. The website was only updated four times a year. If something needed to be changed in a particular record, the editor or associate editor would make that change in the local data files. However, the record would not be changed online until the files were processed for the next update. The separation between editors and the website meant that error correction took longer. Additionally, because new records were only added to the website quarterly, it could take up to three months or longer for items to appear online.

In an ideal world, the *WSB*'s processes and website would have been updated as new and more efficient tools and technologies were developed. However, given the realities of limited (and often shrinking) university department budgets, as well as the economic realities faced by scholarly publication and university presses, the prospect of updating and changing everything to deliver a new *WSB Online* was daunting. As Harner began to think about retirement, he knew that the next editor of the *WSB* would have to be digitally savvy enough to take things to the next level.

In 2013, Texas A&M's Department of English hired Laura Estill, who worked closely with Harner before his retirement during a period that Estill describes as an "apprenticeship" with "a very clear two-year handoff period." For two years, Harner and Estill were credited as co-editors of the *WSB* Online. When Harner retired from Texas A&M, he left the *WSB* entirely in the hands of the new editor. Estill writes, "We could not truly have passed the baton if he had not been willing to let go during the handoff."[231] Estill continues:

> Another way Jim prepared for the handoff was by not imposing his vision on the project. Jim was clear from the start: he knew the site needed updating, but ... he wanted the WSB going forward to reflect my vision and not his, which is why he didn't undertake the much-needed major overhaul before he retired.[232]

Estill envisioned an integrated workflow system for the *WSB*. In this new digital environment, *WSB* graduate assistants, editors, and contributors

---

[231] Laura Estill, "Legacy Technologies and Digital Futures," in *Doing More Digital Humanities: Open Approaches to Creation, Growth, and Development* (Routledge, 2020), 7–24, 13, 14.

[232] Estill, "Legacy Technologies and Digital Futures," 14.

would submit entries in the system. Editors would edit *and* publish entries, which would then become visible to *WSB* users.

Shortly after Estill became editor, the *WSB* secured a grant through Texas A&M's Institute for Digital Humanities and Media Culture to hire Quinn Dombrowski to develop an online submission system for *WSB* editors, graduate assistants, and international contributors.[233] For decades, graduate assistants and international contributors had submitted Microsoft Word documents containing entries, sometimes with byzantine codes (see section 5.1 for an example) that could be riddled with errors. *WSB* editors reviewed the entries, edited them, and coded them using the encoding system developed by Smith and Meserole. Though some of the international contributors knew the encoding system and submitted entries they coded themselves, most of them were unfamiliar with the system. Additionally, *WSB* graduate assistants no longer submitted coded entries. Given that the "WSB's code was an idiosyncratic, non-standard encoding language that contributors would be unable to apply in other DH projects," it didn't make much sense to ask graduate students to spend time learning a nontransferable skill. As Estill recalls, "I found it unethical to ask graduate students to learn *WSB* encoding. Learning programming or encoding is a valuable skill: however, it has diminishing returns if you cannot apply what you've learned."[234] The Drupal-based submission site that Dombrowski set up greatly simplified the submission process for graduate assistants and international contributors, who would no longer be required to submit Word files to *WSB* editors. Though this was a very useful interim submission system, the new "online submission system still had to export in the legacy code," which was "displayed in the old format."[235] Editors were still processing files using the old system and uploading the processed files for the publisher each quarter.

This process changed in 2016 with the release of a new, Drupal-based *WSB* site that integrated the editorial workflow so that the entire process from entry submission to publication was now streamlined into one system,

---

[233] Estill, "Legacy Technologies and Digital Futures," 15.

[234] Estill, "Legacy Technologies and Digital Futures," 14–15.

[235] Estill, "Legacy Technologies and Digital Futures," 15.

making the bibliographic "project more welcoming to new international correspondents," who no longer had to email documents containing entries to *WSB* editors.[236] The new site was more intuitive for users and contributors and greatly facilitated the submission process. Additionally, graduate research assistants were now able to submit their entries directly to editors via the website rather than submitting each entry through a separate form that wasn't part of the website. Each entry waiting to be edited and published was accessible via the back-end of the Drupal-based website, and editors could see the status of each entry in the queue, along with information about who had last saved the entry and timestamps for each entry's revision. Editors were able to submit entries directly into the system, and they were also able to edit submissions from contributors, publishing them directly to the live system without having to wait for an external publisher to upload a new set of entries. Notably, once the entries were published, editors could edit them at any time rather than having to wait until files were processed and uploaded by a programmer with the publisher. Editors now corrected errors as soon as they were found, deleted duplicate entries, added reviews of publications and performances to existing entries as they became available, edited submitted entries directly in the system, and published entries that would go live immediately.

From an editorial perspective, one of the most exciting features of the new system was the ease with which editors added cross-references. Before the 2016 rebuild, cross-referencing was a time-consuming process, and since editors were typing in record numbers for each cross-reference, the probability of producing errors was always a concern. In the new system, the editor started typing the record entry for the cross-reference, and the system auto-completed the bibliographic record to be cross-referenced. Editors then simply clicked on the record to add the cross-reference to the entry, thus hyperlinking the cross-reference within the entry.

---

[236] Estill, "Legacy Technologies and Digital Futures," 16. The rebuild was funded by Texas A&M University's College of Liberal Arts and the Folger Shakespeare Library, working with the Web Development Group (WDG). WDG worked closely with the Folger team, led by Eric Johnson, and *WSB* editorial staff to plan and design the site and its functionality.

The 2016 rebuild also allowed users to access online journal articles and eBooks if the journal or book "is open access or if an institution subscribes to it."[237] Users were now allowed to access their subscribing institution's holdings by simply clicking on a "Find Text" button. Users were able to "click directly from a book collection to each of its chapters" and "click on journal titles, author names, or tags to browse more organically."[238] The *WSB* was now integrated "with multiple citation management systems such as EndNote or Zotero," and the site was "mobile-friendly" and "navigable from a phone or tablet."[239]

The rebuild also included new taxonomic terms for classifying each bibliographic record. As Estill explains:

> The WSB is the most comprehensive bibliography of Shakespeare scholarship: we carefully reconsidered our taxonomy of how articles are classified, which involved thinking about the landscape of Shakespeare studies and how it is divided. Of course, any project considering changing their taxonomy needs to ensure that it can update old entries with new labels or accept loss of functionality. We added "musical score" as a document type that is separate from "monograph." We also renamed "computer software" to "digital project." These changes are not just about keeping up with current nomenclature: they are about accurately reflecting a field of study.[240]

Notably, Estill's reflections on rethinking the classification of entries echo Smith and Meserole's negotiations during the early days of computerizing *WSB* data: how do we create a digital system that is flexible enough to accommodate strict bibliographic standards and to allow for changes over time?

---

[237] Estill, "Legacy Technologies and Digital Futures," 17.
[238] Estill, "Legacy Technologies and Digital Futures," 17.
[239] Estill, "Legacy Technologies and Digital Futures," 17.
[240] Estill, "Legacy Technologies and Digital Futures," 17–18.

5.5 Continuing the World Shakespeare Bibliography, 2016–present

In 2019, Heidi Craig joined the *WSB* as Editor, while Estill shifted to an advisory role. Craig was joined by two new *WSB* Associate Editors, Katayoun Torabi (2018–2020) and Dorothy Todd (2020–2023). During that same year, Oxford University Press became the publisher of the *WSB* and *Shakespeare Quarterly*. While maintaining the practices of finding, annotating and publishing entries in the format established in the 2016 site rebuild, the team also turned its attention to public outreach and publication.[241] The editorial team created a Resources page, which featured tools the team created to aid researchers, instructors, and students, including an online how-to tutorial and a teaching handout with ideas on how to incorporate the *WSB* into the university classroom, outlining exercises such as in-class group annotation for the *WSB* as well as a *WSB* annotation assignment for individual students.[242]

The timing of the team's shift to questions of access and outreach was fortuitous, as such matters became especially urgent during the COVID-19 pandemic that engulfed the globe starting in early 2020. The pandemic transformed work life for people across the world and revealed the material resources, processes, and workflows that the *WSB*'s seamless digital interface often obscured. For instance, the *WSB* relies on library services in order to obtain the materials to annotate, and the pandemic disrupted library services and operations not only at its home Texas A&M Libraries, but at libraries worldwide. Of course, remote operations were nothing new for the *WSB*: graduate students and staff were used to working away from the office at various points throughout the semester. The difference, though, was that this time, the entire *WSB* team – the editor, associate editors, undergraduate interns, and graduate student research assistants – had to shift to working remotely with very little time (if any) spent in the office for

---

[241] Publications emerging from this effort include Heidi Craig and Laura Estill, "Browse as Interface"; Craig and Estill, "Finding and Accessing Shakespeare Scholarship in the Global South: Digital Research and Bibliography," in *Digital Shakespeares from the Global South*, ed. Amrita Sen (Palgrave, 2022), 17–36; and Craig, Estill, and May, "A Rationale of Trans-Inclusive Bibliography."

[242] Craig, Estill, May, and Katayoun Torabi, www.worldshakesbib.org/resources.

almost a year. Nevertheless, its long-standing digital format and flexible workflows that capitalized on digital resources (such as online articles and eBooks) meant the *WSB* was in a good position to weather the storm and even create new research opportunities.[243]

As a resource that annotates performances from the theater (an industry devastated by the pandemic), the *WSB* was attuned to the theater industry's adaptations. For a time, in-person stage productions around the world were halted due to pandemic restrictions, and many theaters moved their productions online. Of course, online productions of Shakespeare's plays were not new in 2020. However, there were some new things for the *WSB* staff to consider as they composed entries for these productions and considered particular questions about the performances. Was a production "staged" online with the actors Zoom-ing in from different locations? Did the actors appear on a theater's physical stage without an audience in the same physical location as the actors? Was a performance recorded and the video recording made available for streaming (via a platform like YouTube) for a certain period of time (either for free or by purchasing tickets)? Should the performance be classified as a "stage production" or as a "film"? The *WSB* staff considered a variety of new questions involving the nuance of each performance in order to determine the most useful bibliographic data to include for each performance entry.[244] The team also started to tag performances touched by the pandemic, such as Shakespeare performances that suddenly shifted online or which were expressly designed for a digital format during the COVID-19 era.[245] The team additionally tagged the

---

[243] The *WSB* team presented its paper on trans-inclusive bibliography at several international conferences hosted online, enabling us to convey our ideas to a global audience without ever leaving home.

[244] For more about the COVID-19 pandemic and virtual performances of Shakespeare, see Gemma Kate Allred, Benjamin Broadribb, and Erin Sullivan, eds., *Lockdown Shakespeare: New Evolutions in Performance and Adaptation*, *Shakespeare and Adaptation*, The Arden Shakespeare (Bloomsbury, 2022).

[245] Sarah Hatchuel, "Co-vidding Shakespeare: Creating Collective Videos from Shakespeare's Plays during the COVID-19 Pandemic," *Angles: New Perspectives on the Anglophone World* 12 (2021), doi.org/10.4000/angles.3415.

many articles about Shakespearean connections to the pandemic, whether about how Shakespearean theater professionals were grappling with and adapting to theater closures, how Shakespeare served as solace, or even inspiration, with his creative activity during early modern plague times potentially providing lessons for people who were currently experiencing lockdown.[246] As always, the *WSB* remained focused on providing research resources to Shakespeareans.

In 2023, the *World Shakespeare Bibliography*'s editorial operations shifted with Heidi Craig to the University of Toronto, Scarborough, thanks to the vision and support of Dr. Patricia Akhimie, Director of the Folger Institute, which funded several new student research fellowships to assist with the *WSB*'s compilation and publication. By 2024, the *WSB*'s content management system was due for an upgrade. The Folger's head of Information Technology, Seán Stickle, spearheaded a migration of the *WSB* from Drupal to a WordPress site, maintaining the site's design and functionality but with a decidedly more user-friendly back-end for editors and other contributors. From index cards and early forms of computerization, to CD-ROMs, to Drupal and WordPress sites; from Penn State, to Texas A&M, to the remote workspaces of the pandemic, to the Folger, to the University of Toronto, these various technical shifts and institutional changes demonstrate that even long-standing resources and practices must change and adapt over time to sustain a project this large and complex. And yet, the constant for the *WSB* has been to provide the fullest records about Shakespeare performance and scholarship to a global audience.

As this Element has shown, the history of the *WSB* reflects the broader history of Shakespearean bibliography: the way we find our scholarship and reflect on our field of study is through collaboration between human

---

[246] See for instance, Stephanie Gearhart, ""Because Survival is Insufficient': Sir Patrick Stewart's #ASonnetADay and the Role of Adaptation in a Pandemic," *Borrowers and Lenders: The Journal of Shakespeare and Appropriation* 13, no. 3 (2021), borrowers-ojs-azsu.tdl.org/borrowers/article/view/327/604; Emma Smith, "What Shakespeare Teaches Us about Living with Pandemics." *New York Times* March 28, 2020, www.nytimes.com/2020/03/28/opinion/coronavirus-shakespeare.html.

ingenuity and technological transformations. As we look to the past, we also look to the future, with hope and anticipation about how Shakespearean bibliography will continue to evolve.

Coda: Looking Forward

Bibliographies are the work of bibliographers, that is, people. These reference works are shaped by the people who compile them, the access to information and sources those people enjoy, and the institutional, regional, and national contexts in which they are compiled. For decades, W. W. Greg's quotation, copied and framed by James L. Harner (Figure 10), hung on the *World Shakespeare Bibliography* office wall, calling bibliographers "useful drudges" and "servi a biblioteca," that is, servants to the library, and ultimately, the discipline. Today, Shakespeare bibliography is always undertaken collaboratively: whether with co-editors working on a given project, or by turning to existing bibliographies, whether to find information or omissions.

As human-created reference works, bibliographies are the result of choices: the scope and organizational structure of a bibliography will foreground some works while pushing others to the margin or eliding them, making them undiscoverable. The ways we categorize and tag items in a bibliography necessarily reflect a given point of view and scholarly moment. These decisions can often look neutral or objective, obscuring more fraught political, cultural, and technological realities. And even within well-defined ambits and with perfectly curated and navigable taxonomies, there will be omissions. Bibliographies have the potential to control what seems important in a given field, and Shakespeare studies is no exception. This Element argues for the importance of bibliographies in both shaping and reflecting scholarly practice; bibliographies, then, are valuable artifacts to produce, interrogate, and evaluate.

In our current age of algorithmic and automatic list-making, it is precisely that automation that has led to an explosion of misinformation and AI-generated junk. With the rise of artificial intelligence, Shakespearean bibliography continues to require human intervention and expertise to tame the "genial dragon" of bibliography.[247] While algorithms

---

[247] Habenicht, "Shakespeare: An Annotated World Bibliography for 1973," 441.

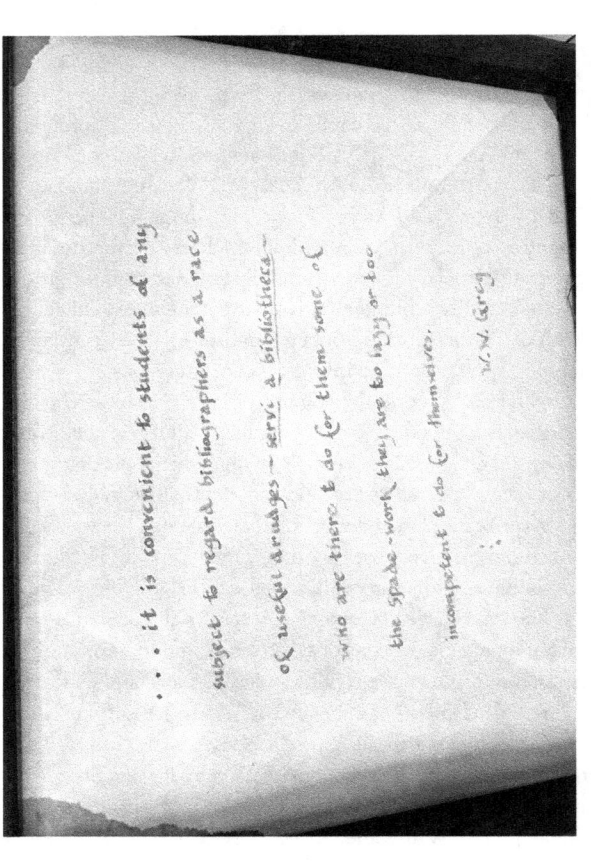

Figure 10 W. W. Greg quotation from the *World Shakespeare Bibliography* office, copied and framed by James L. Harner: "... it is convenient to students of any subject to regard bibliographers as a race of useful drudges – servi a bibliotheca – who are there to do for them some of the spade-work they are too lazy or too incompetent to do for themselves. W. W. Greg"

can certainly find pieces of digitized text faster than a human, it still takes a human eye to evaluate and organize the content. Artificial intelligence can even offer summaries of texts that it "reads," but it does not understand what it reads, and it cannot see the contexts and biases of what it ingests.

Even before the onslaught of artificial intelligence, bibliographers had to use their judgment when it came to including questionable scholarship produced by the rise of paper mills and pay-to-publish predatory journals. Now, as artificial intelligence spews virtual reams of textual slop, bibliographers will be faced with an even more Sisyphean task when it comes to separating the wheat from the chaff. While these virtual reams of AI-generated text are not tangible, we know they are taking a real toll on the environment. Shakespeare has long been a daunting field of study to enter, as students and newcomers face the task of catching up on centuries of humanist inquiry. Bibliographies are a record of scholarship that can offer a glimpse into the scholarly preoccupations of a moment; while no bibliography is complete or unbiased, the best bibliographies can support equity and increase visibility by making multilingual criticism, translations, editions, and performances searchable, as well as bringing new or overlooked voices into the scholarly conversation. Bibliographies are lifelines: some with annotations, some with specialized areas of focus, and some helping us stay abreast of recent publications.

This Element has focused on a particular kind of Shakespeare bibliography: enumerative bibliographies of scholarship about Shakespeare. While we have touched on a number of bibliographies, both periodical and omnibus, the hundreds of bibliographies beyond the scope of this Element invite further study. These Shakespeare bibliographies offer records of our research that in turn shapes how we continue to research. Bibliographies make work findable and help us tell the story of our discipline.

Ultimately, the history of Shakespeare bibliography is important because it helps us better navigate the (increasingly online) scholarly resources available to us in the present. Moreover, Shakespearean bibliographies offer a record of past and present scholarship, which can itself shape future scholarship. We hope this Element prompts scholars to think about enumerative projects not as monolithic reference works, but rather, as purposefully constructed lists that are necessarily incomplete and reflect the contexts and decisions that went into their creation as well as the technologies with which they were created. In Shakespeare studies, as with research more broadly, we cannot effectively search for information unless we know the ambit of the material we search, why it was gathered, and how it was arranged.

Acknowledgments and Collaborations

We would like to thank our research assistants who worked on this project: Minjung Ha (Texas A&M University), Alexandra LaGrand (Texas A&M University), and Alex Lambourne (St. Francis Xavier University). Thanks also to those who spoke to Kris as we pieced together the *World Shakespeare Bibliography*'s recent history: Darinda Harner, Priscilla J. Letterman Meserole, and John B. Smith. Thanks to Jochen Ruebener for translations from German.

All four authors contributed equally to this Element; any author can be listed as the first author in citations.

We are grateful for funding from the Canada Research Chairs Program, the Social Sciences and Humanities Research Council of Canada Institutional Grant at St. Francis Xavier University, and the College of Arts and Sciences at Texas A&M University to make this volume open access. We would also like to thank the Department of English at Texas A&M University for funding to secure image permissions.

This book is dedicated to the memory of Jim Harner and to the perseverance of all bibliographers, including those who often go unacknowledged and unnamed.

Cambridge Elements

Shakespeare and Text

Claire M. L. Bourne
The Pennsylvania State University

Claire M. L. Bourne is Associate Professor of English at The Pennsylvania State University. She is author of *Typographies of Performance in Early Modern England* (Oxford University Press 2020) and editor of the collection *Shakespeare / Text* (Bloomsbury 2021). She has published extensively on early modern book design and reading practices in venues such as *PBSA*, *ELR*, *Shakespeare*, and numerous edited collections. She is also co-author (with Jason Scott-Warren) of an article attributing the annotations in the Free Library of Philadelphia's copy of the Shakespeare First Folio to John Milton. She has edited Fletcher and Massinger's *The Sea Voyage* for the *Routledge Anthology of Early Modern Drama* (2020) and is working on an edition of *Henry the Sixth, Part 1* for the Arden Shakespeare, Fourth Series.

Rory Loughnane
University of Kent

Rory Loughnane is Reader in Early Modern Studies and Co-director of the Centre for Medieval and Early Modern Studies at the University of Kent. He is the author or editor of nine books and has published widely on Shakespeare and textual studies. In his role as Associate Editor of the New Oxford Shakespeare, he has edited more than ten of Shakespeare's plays, and co-authored with Gary Taylor a book-length study about the 'Canon and Chronology' of Shakespeare's works. He is a General Editor of the forthcoming

Oxford Marlowe edition, a Series Editor of Studies in Early
Modern Authorship (Routledge), a General Editor of the
CADRE database (cadredb.net), and a General Editor of The
Revels Plays series (Manchester University Press).

ADVISORY BOARD

Patricia Akhimie
The Folger Institute
Terri Bourus
Florida State University
Dennis Britton
*University of British
  Columbia*
Miles P. Grier
*Queen's College,
  City University
  of New York*
Chiaki Hanabusa
Keio University
Sujata Iyengar
University of Georgia
Jason Scott-Warren
University of Cambridge

M. J. Kidnie
University of Western Ontario
Zachary Lesser
University of Pennsylvania
Tara L. Lyons
Illinois State University
Joyce MacDonald
University of Kentucky
Laurie Maguire
*Magdalen College, University
  of Oxford*
David McInnis
University of Melbourne
Iolanda Plescia
Sapienza – University of Rome
Alan Stewart
Columbia University

About the Series
Cambridge Elements in Shakespeare and Text offers a platform for
original scholarship about the creation, circulation, reception,
remaking, use, performance, teaching, and translation of the
Shakespearean text across time and place. The series seeks to publish
research that challenges–and pushes beyond–the conventional
parameters of Shakespeare and textual studies.

Cambridge Elements

Shakespeare and Text

ELEMENTS IN THE SERIES

Shakespeare, Malone and the Problems of Chronology
Tiffany Stern

Theatre History, Attribution Studies, and the Question of Evidence
Holger Schott Syme

Facsimiles and the History of Shakespeare Editing
Paul Salzman

Editing Archipelagic Shakespeare
Rory Loughnane and Willy Maley

Shakespeare Broadcasts and the Question of Value
Beth Sharrock

Shakespeare and Scale: The Archive of Early Printed English
Anupam Basu

Textual Genealogies and Shakespeare's History Plays
Gary Taylor and John Nance

Anne Shakespeare's Epitaph
Katherine West Scheil

Collaboration, Technologies, and the History of Shakespearean Bibliography
Heidi Craig, Laura Estill, Kris L. May, and Dorothy Todd

A full series listing is available at: www.cambridge.org/ESTX

For EU product safety concerns, contact us at Calle de José Abascal, 56–1°,
28003 Madrid, Spain or eugpsr@cambridge.org.

www.ingramcontent.com/pod-product-compliance
Lightning Source LLC
LaVergne TN
LVHW011845060526
838200LV00054B/4168